W9-AKZ-797

THE POLITICAL LEGACY OF
George D. Aiken

George D. Aiken at a Senate Foreign Relations Committee hearing, December 1970. Courtesy of Bailey/Howe Library, University of Vermont.

THE POLITICAL LEGACY OF

George D. Aiken

Wise Old Owl of the

U.S. Senate

EDITED BY

Michael Sherman

Foreword by Mike Mansfield

Vermont Historical Society
Montpelier, Vermont

The Countryman Press, Inc.
Woodstock, Vermont

BENNINGTON FREE LIBRARY

Copyright © 1995 Vermont Historical Society
Foreword copyright © 1995 by Mike Mansfield

Published by The Countryman Press, Inc., Woodstock, Vermont 05091
in association with Vermont Historical Society, Montpelier, Vermont 05609

All rights reserved. No part of this book may be reproduced in any form or by any
electronic or mechanical means including information storage and retrieval systems
without permission in writing from the publisher, except by a reviewer who
may quote brief passages.

LIBRARY OF CONGRESS CATALOGING–IN–PUBLICATION DATA

The political legacy of George D. Aiken, wise old owl of the U.S. Senate /
Michael Sherman, editor; foreword by Mike Mansfield.
p.   cm.
Includes bibliographical references (p. 175) and index.
ISBN 0-88150-352-5
1. Aiken, George D. (George David), 1892–1984. 2. Legislators–United
States–Biography. 3. United States. Congress. Senate–Biography.
I. Sherman, Michael, 1944- .
E748.A193P65 1995
328.73'092–dc20
[B]
95-3953
CIP

Cover design by James Brisson
Text formatting and design by Karen Savary

Printed in the United States of America
10 9 8 7 6 5 4 3 2 1

528.73
pol 96
2.

Contents

Foreword

GEORGE AIKEN WILL ALWAYS BE REMEMBERED WITH fondness and affection. A longtime member of the U.S. Senate, he was independent in his outlook, considerate of his fellow senators, and appreciative of the difficulties under which that body worked. He was a man of honesty, decency, patriotism, and dedication to his country and to his home state of Vermont.

Serving more than four decades in the U.S. Senate, Aiken made substantial contributions to its functionings and helped define it in post–World War II America. He had an unblemished reputation for dealing fairly with his colleagues, showing both compassion and understanding. He always remembered that several points of view are possible in political debates, and his open-mindedness in confronting the issues led to a reputation for integrity and independence. He had the respect of both parties and was regarded as an example for other senators to follow.

In a chamber noted for its loquacity, Aiken's succinctness was legendary. He was not ego driven but a man of the people—a "farmer," as he described himself—a man of wisdom people listened to, a man who swayed others because they looked to him for guidance. His sound intelligence, great tolerance, and sensitivity characterized his life in the Senate.

His state and his country trusted him implicitly, and he repaid them for that trust with his diligence, dedication, and devotion. Although Vermont rightly claimed him as its own, the entire nation respected, admired, and benefited from his many contributions to its political tradition.

George Aiken was a man for his time and a man for all times. He was a great senator and a man who made our country a better nation in which to live.

Mike Mansfield

Acknowledgments

*T*HIS BOOK, LIKE ALL SUCH UNDERTAKINGS, IS the product of many hands and many minds. Some of those who contributed to its production and publication will be obvious to the reader. Several who would otherwise remain invisible must also be acknowledged for their contributions.

The authors of the works that follow, of course, deserve the first thanks. They not only prepared their original presentations but gave the editor wide latitude to do his job and, mostly without grumbling at the additional work, rewrote sentences or paragraphs, suffered deletions and an occasional expansion of their original paper, added endnotes, and patiently explained to the editor what should have been all too clear.

Two authors whose contributions to the 1991 Aiken lectures do not appear here must also be acknowledged. Robert T. Stafford, former governor of Vermont and former U.S. senator from Vermont, served as a commentator for one session of the lectures. His reminiscences and recollections of George D. Aiken as his predecessor in the governor's office and colleague in the Senate threw many spotlights on Aiken's career, elaborating and, for the most part, corroborating both the details and broad outlines of Aiken's public life presented by the other speakers.

Robert Bothwell, professor of history at the University of

Toronto, Canada, presented a paper, "Seeing Canada as It Really Is." That paper provided the context for understanding Aiken's long and often lonely commitment to forging strong diplomatic, economic, and political ties with Vermont's and the United States' northern neighbor. Professor Bothwell skillfully reviewed the tangled and confused web of misinterpretations and lack of interpretation of Canadian history and politics that Aiken inherited and worked hard to overcome during his career in the Senate. Charles O'Brien's contribution to this collection refers to Professor Bothwell's presentation, which constraints of economy and the decision to focus on Aiken's career prevent us from offering here.

Several months after the 1991 Aiken lectures, an editorial advisory board convened to discuss publication of these papers. Howard Ball, dean of the College of Arts and Sciences, University of Vermont; Samuel B. Hand, professor of history at the University of Vermont; Connell Gallagher, assistant director of libraries for research at the University of Vermont; Constance McGovern, at that time associate provost of the University of Vermont, now provost at Frostburg State College, Frostburg, Maryland; and Stephen Terry, vice president for external affairs at Green Mountain Power Corporation, provided advice, guidance, comments on editorial decisions, and encouragement. I especially thank Sam Hand for asking me to be the editor of this book, helping me with information about Vermont politics, filling in the gaps in my knowledge of American diplomatic history, collaborating with me to write the introduction and—with his wry and enigmatic good humor—keeping close watch on its progress.

The Publications Committee and Board of Trustees of the Vermont Historical Society took this publication under their wing and encouraged me to undertake the editing of the Aiken lectures as part of my work for the society. Their decision to support this project acknowledges not only George Aiken's important place in Vermont history but also the society's role in contributing to and promoting scholarship that has national as well as regional significance.

Carl Taylor of Countryman Press enthusiastically endorsed a collaborative publication. Without his help and the help of his staff, this book would have been a much different, less elegant, and less accessible volume.

I owe special thanks to Reidun Nuquist, who has prepared an index that enhances the usefulness of this collection for scholars and casual readers alike; to Jeffrey Marshall of the University of Vermont's Bailey/Howe Library special collections department, who assisted me with the selection and inclusion of photographs of George Aiken from the Aiken Papers; and to the University of Vermont's audiovisual services, which videotaped the entire lecture series in 1991 and provided video transcripts of speeches.

Alice Colwell, the Vermont Historical Society's managing editor, deserves special thanks. She meticulously copyedited the essays after I thought I had done most of the work to make them accessible to their new audience. The small forest of notes and queries she affixed to the manuscript sent me scurrying to the library for additional facts and to my medicine cabinet for headache relief, but they helped me make this book more coherent, more useful to the present and future generations of scholars, and more pleasurable for all of us to read. Lola Aiken, whose dedication to the Aiken lecture series is noted in the Introduction and whose role in her late husband's public career is noted many times in these papers, also helped this book come into being. No project that examines and interprets George Aiken's career escapes her notice, fails to win her support, or can miss taking into account her significant contributions to his work.

Michael Sherman

Introduction
Samuel B. Hand and Michael Sherman

O N FEBRUARY 14, 1974, GEORGE D. AIKEN, DEAN OF
the U.S. Senate, announced that he would not seek
reelection after forty-four consecutive years in elective
office. First elected to the Vermont state legislature in 1930, he
went on to serve as House speaker, lieutenant governor, and governor of Vermont. In 1940 he was elected to the U.S. Senate. A
lifelong Republican, Aiken left office with an enviable reputation
for sagacity and independence. His close friend and colleague in
the Senate, Mike Mansfield (D–Mont.), said of him during the
often acrimonious debate on the war in Southeast Asia that he was
neither a hawk nor a dove but a "wise old owl." The characteriza-
tion stuck and became part of Aiken's political identity.

In 1974, friends and admirers seeking to honor Aiken with a
permanent tribute conceived and endowed the George D. Aiken
Lectures, sponsored by the University of Vermont. The Aiken
Lectures usually alternate among the areas of foreign affairs, energy, and agriculture, subjects on which Senator Aiken was particularly well informed and active in his public life. The George D.
Aiken Lectures board of directors includes the president of the
university as ex officio chair and the deans of the Colleges of Arts
and Sciences, Agriculture, and Business and Engineering, who act

as chairpersons of the program committee on a rotating basis. Other members are Lola P. Aiken, whose unflagging dedication to the Aiken Lectures and the memory of her late husband has been a fixed star; Elizabeth Quinn and Steve Terry, both of whom served on Aiken's Senate staff; Lieutenant Governor Barbara Snelling, whose vision as a UVM vice president helped establish the series; and, when this series was presented, the late Robert Mitchell, publisher and editor of the *Rutland Herald*.

The "Aiken Legacy," the fourteenth Aiken Lecture Series, presented October 24–26, 1991, was the first to focus on George D. Aiken the man. All of the programs before and since have concentrated on areas of interest to Aiken. The full roster of lectures follows:

1975 International Affairs
1976 Social and Economic Problems of Rural Societies
1977 Energy
1978 The United States and Africa: Toward a New Relationship
1979 Our Food: Cash, Calories, and Controversy
1980 Nuclear Energy
1981 Mass Media and Foreign Policy
1982 Landscapes and Landowners: Private Needs and Public Interests
1983 Acid Precipitation
1985 Nuclear Weapons and American Foreign Policy
1986 Competing Visions of Vermont: Agriculture, Communities, and Groundwater
1988 Economic Development
1990 Solving Environmental Problems Through Technology
1991 The Aiken Legacy
1992 The Northern Forest
1993 Human Genetics: Navigating the New Frontier

As it planned for the 1991 lectures, the program committee concluded that it was time for a symposium on Aiken himself. In honoring the pledge that the lectures constitute a permanent tribute to Aiken, the committee decided it was appropriate to acquaint a new generation with Aiken—who he was and why we celebrate his memory. Students entering college in 1991 were barely a year old when Aiken retired; their historical memory seldom reached back to 1975. Possibly because of the presence of a building named for Aiken on the University of Vermont campus, Aiken had become as much a place as a person. The committee would not have scheduled the symposium, however, and this book would not have been offered to the public, if a sounding of national scholars had not revealed the sentiment that sufficient time had passed and sufficient sources had become available to make some tentative assessments of Aiken's career and historical significance. This volume provides a collection of those judgments.

First, let us sketch in some details of Aiken's political career. He entered state politics in 1931 as the representative from Putney (population 835) and distinguished himself by helping defeat a flood control proposal authorizing private utility companies to construct storage reservoirs and generate hydroelectric power at dam sites throughout Vermont. The bill was sponsored by the House speaker and had the support of the private utilities but was blocked by those who urged the state to "protect the people ... from giving to public service corporations ... our beautiful and fertile valleys." Aiken championed the opposition. His membership on the House Conservation and Development Committee, to which the flood control bill was assigned, assured the plan's demise.

Aiken's efforts to defeat the flood control plan elevated him to unaccustomed prominence; after the November 1932 elections, when the speaker was upset in his race for reelection to the House, Aiken declared his own candidacy for House speaker. His opponent was a Barre banker, and 1933, as Aiken wryly noted, was a good year to run against a banker. He won handily. With both feet planted firmly on the ladder of political succession, he climbed to the position of lieutenant governor in 1934. In 1936, when

Governor Charles Smith chose to retire after a single term, Aiken was elected governor.

So rapid a rise was rare. Aiken's opportunities were heightened by the depression and his uncanny gift to personify qualities Vermont rhetoric acclaimed as virtues. He embodied precisely those traditions the state most liked about itself. He was, he boasted, "born and ... always lived on a hillside farm among a people who for two hundred years have handed down certain attitudes of mind from generation to generation. Some folks call us old-fashioned and backward-looking for adhering to the ideals and principles characteristic of the people who settled our State."[1]

A partisan Republican, he nonetheless maintained that Roosevelt's New Deal offered substantial benefits. Vermonters, Aiken alleged, did not fear experimentation but had "the sense to drop experiments that failed."[2] He had supported a state income tax and state highway system acts and had lavished praise on some particular New Deal agencies. Unrelentingly critical of Republicans who instinctively rejected all New Deal programs, he promised he would never oppose "any measure calculated to relieve human distress ... simply because those measures are endorsed by an opposing party."[3] Still, Aiken thought Franklin Roosevelt represented a disturbing drift toward greater federal and executive power, and Vermont's spirit of liberty and self-reliance prompted eternal vigilance against the "type of centralized government which history has so often proved undesirable."[4]

Despite Aiken's explicit sympathy for much of the New Deal, his gubernatorial administrations (1937–1941) confirmed the image of Vermont's steadfast Republicanism. In 1936 Vermont and Maine had been the only states to vote against Roosevelt, and Aiken devoted substantial time and effort as governor to resisting a New Deal plan to construct a Connecticut River Valley Authority modeled after the Tennessee Valley Authority. As one of the few Republicans to withstand the 1936 Democratic landslide, the Vermont governor was closely monitored in the national press. Aiken balanced his resistance to greater federal control with a positive and compassionate vision of Republicanism; his rhetoric was imbued with a moral force that appealed within and beyond Vermont's borders. Appalled at the thought that the federal government would flood his cherished hill farm to provide electric power for the cities of southern New England, he fought to save Vermonters' "right to breathe and think and act freely and naturally."5 He repeatedly called for protecting Vermont's natural resources against the encroachments of the New Deal and the private utilities alike, at the same time demanding a "new Republicanism" that recognized the needs of the working class and accepted active government without the need for deficit spending or executive aggrandizement.

Aiken's lonely eminence as a Republican governor and his successes at frustrating New Deal hydropower efforts thrust him into the role of national party spokesman. In a nationally broadcast 1938 Lincoln Day address and again in his book *Speaking from Vermont,* Aiken castigated "old guard" Republican party leaders who were, he claimed, too wedded to corporate and monied interests. He challenged them to become more responsive to the needs of voters.

Such public pronouncements—so popular among rank-and-file Republicans that they helped launch an Aiken-for-president boomlet—completely alienated the national and Vermont party organizations. Fearing that Aiken might seek a third term for governor in 1940, the state's Republican Committee took the unprecedented step of endorsing a candidate almost a year prior to the Republican primary. Aiken's aspirations lay elsewhere, however. In June 1940 U.S. Senator Ernest W. Gibson died, and Aiken appointed his son, Ernest Gibson Jr., as interim senator. Aiken's close friend and political ally, Ernest Gibson Jr. declined to seek election. Aiken declared his own candidacy and captured the Republican primary from Ralph Flanders. Elected in November 1940, he spent the next thirty-four years in the U.S. Senate.

The essays that follow illuminate several facets of Aiken's career in the Senate, as well as the changes within the institution itself and the developments in national and international relations that framed the context of his three decades of service in Congress.

It is well to identify at the outset some themes that run throughout the history of Aiken's years in public life.

First, Aiken never entertained the notion that there were permanent or perfect solutions. He frequently drew on an anecdote from his youth to temper the enthusiasm of political reformers. For many years a large boulder in the middle of one of his father's fields complicated the plowing and harvesting. Finally, one autumn, Aiken's father relented to pleas and arguments to remove the boulder, assembled a large group of friends and neighbors, and after much struggle hauled the boulder away. When Aiken and his father returned to the field to do the spring plowing, they found that the frost heaves had thrown up a new boulder in exactly the spot where they had removed its predecessor. "We gained about four square feet," he mused. Translating this into political terms, Aiken once commented that we should enact legislation conscious of how it might be applied by our enemies, as our friends do not last forever and we cannot be sure who will be in office ten years from now.

Second, Aiken was a stalwart Republican who voted consistently with his party. He earned his reputation as a maverick almost entirely in intraparty disputes, where he often attempted to redirect party policy. He believed he could exercise his greatest influence within Republican party councils. His role in the controversial Taft-Hartley Act (1947) is probably the best illustration of his staunch Republicanism. He fought with limited success in committee against many of the act's provisions and went so far as to predict that if Congress passed punitive labor legislation, the Republicans would be defeated in the 1948 elections. Yet he voted for the bill, then voted to override President Harry Truman's veto. Although he considered the bill far from perfect, he justified his votes by assuming that his loyalty to the party would entitle him to a voice in amending the bill at some future date.

A third theme evident from the earliest days of his political career was Aiken's fear of the growth of federal and in particular executive power. This concern was foreshadowed in his disputes with the supporters of hydropower when he was state legislator and governor and continued in his opposition to lend-lease in his first months as a U.S. senator. In debates of the 1957 and 1960 Civil Rights Acts, he was against granting the Justice Department the authority to create an assistant attorney general for civil rights who would wield ambiguously defined powers. "One of our greatest struggles," he commented in 1957, "is the fight against encroachment ... by the Federal Government to gain control over State, Community, and local affairs."6

Fourth, Aiken spoke and wrote of Vermont history often and was very much aware that the state was created out of a struggle over property rights. He probably would have agreed that property rights were the guardian of every other right, not in the crass sense but in the historic sense—in the tradition of John Locke and Thomas Jefferson, who argued that property ownership established the economic basis for freedom from government coercion and the enjoyment of liberty. Proud that Vermont's 1777 constitution was the first to provide that "property ought to be subservient to public uses when necessity requires it" (chapter 1, article 2), he nevertheless insisted that government respect the other provision in the same article, that "whenever any person's property is taken for the use of the public, the owner ought to receive an equivalent of money." He brought this same principle to debates over the Public Accommodations Act of 1964. In his famous "Mrs. Murphy's boardinghouse" compromise, he persuaded his Republican colleagues that by excluding establishments that housed five or fewer individuals, Congress could simultaneously maintain traditional political rights and accomplish its larger objective of prohibiting discrimination in public accommodations on the basis of race.

These four principles—pragmatism, party loyalty, caution about the limits of government to solve problems, and respect for tradition—were the major strands in the network of values that influenced Aiken and his political decisions. The chapters that follow demonstrate how Aiken put these principles to work.

The essays in this book appear in a different order than they did in the October 1991 program. In the first two essays, the authors explore the political environment in which Aiken matured and operated. James Wright probes Aiken's roots in New England's Progressive movement and culture, which Aiken acknowledged to have had a lifelong influence on his own political philosophy and public career. Herbert S. Parmet, looking back from Aiken's time in the U.S. Senate, shows how the senator's values were buffeted by Republican party politics in the second half of the twentieth century.

The next three essays examine Aiken's career as a U.S. senator. Donald A. Ritchie provides a context for Aiken's long service (1941–1975) by discussing three decades of institutional change within the Senate. Stephen C. Terry gives a staff member's perspective on Aiken's daily routine, revealing how the working day of a senator weaves together personal and philosophical priorities, constituency concerns, and the highly politicized negotiations of a deliberative body. Anna Kasten Nelson builds on Terry's view by emphasizing how senators interact to forge major policy decisions within a bipolar environment of politics and statecraft.

Three essays discuss Aiken's contributions to U.S. foreign policy in the post–World War II era. Thomas G. Paterson summarizes the country's changing role in foreign policy culminating in the war in Southeast Asia. Mark Stoler details the extent and limitations of Aiken's influence upon that foreign policy, with particular attention to Aiken's dissent from U.S. involvement in Southeast Asia. Charles F. O'Brien discusses Aiken's long-standing commitment to the important but seldom-reported U.S. relationship with Canada.

The volume concludes with three personal reminiscences. D. Gregory Sanford, who worked with Aiken on the oral history project after the senator's retirement from politics, discusses the significance and potential uses of the University of Vermont's oral history and manuscript collections. These, Sanford attests, provide an additional level of resources, beyond the public and published records, for knowing Aiken the man and politician. Former Vermont governor Philip H. Hoff records three episodes of working with Senator Aiken that demonstrate many of the complexities of state and federal cooperation compounded by interparty tensions. The final piece, by Judge James L. Oakes, is an eloquent and highly personal tribute to the life and career of George Aiken and those qualities that made him such a respected and endearing figure in state and national politics.

There are some inherent dangers in presenting as published essays works that were conceived as oral presentations. We have attempted to adapt the informality of the spoken word to the requirements of the printed page while retaining the often personal engagement of the speaker with Aiken the man and Aiken the political figure. We recognize, too, that the rapport that grows up between speakers and the audience, especially over a three-day conference, cannot be recaptured in a book that will be read and used as a collection of essays. The audience itself, therefore, presents an interesting editorial problem.

Many of those who assembled at the University of Vermont in 1991 to hear about Aiken either knew him personally or knew enough about him, his career, and his times to relieve the speakers of the responsibility of providing biographical background about those closely associated with Aiken's public career in Vermont and in Washington, D.C. In addressing the needs of a different audience, we have attempted to supply some of the identifying information that speakers and audience brought into the lecture hall.

One particularly nettlesome problem, for example, was how to refer to George Aiken in this book. For most of his years in Congress, Senator Aiken liked to be called "Governor." In most of the presentations at the conference, therefore, speakers talked about the "governor" in the U.S. Senate. The opportunities for confusion here were legion, and we have chosen to eliminate Aiken's self-selected honorific title for those years when he was no longer the governor of Vermont.

The reader will find in this book some contradictions and differences in interpretation of Aiken's career and the political environment in which he worked. The reader will also find some repetition of facts and events that were crucial for understanding and interpreting Aiken's life and career. These, too, are the inevitable consequences of transforming a conference—especially a conference of Aiken's friends, colleagues, and admirers—into a book of essays that will be useful for a wider audience of readers and researchers, some of whom may have more critical and certainly more detached perspectives on Aiken's career or the history of politics and U.S. political institutions. We have tried to eliminate some of the redundancies, but because many of the authors use the same event or set of relationships to characterize and epitomize Aiken's career, doing away with all repetition would have impoverished some contributions. When interpretations varied or contradicted one another, we made no attempt to resolve these differences but instead leave it to the reader to assess the accuracy, validity, or usefulness of each piece.

Finally, we acknowledge the passage of time between the occasion when these lectures were composed and delivered and when they became a published collection. In that interval some crucial events in U.S. and world history have taken place that may cast new light on how Aiken viewed the world, how his perspective corresponds with contemporary reality, and what we may learn from his career. To take only two of the most persistent themes in this collection—foreign policy and party politics—it will perhaps belabor the obvious but is certainly necessary to note that since 1991 the cold war has ended and the United States faces new problems and issues in its relationships with the successor states of the Soviet Union. This in turn has implications for how the United States sees its role in international politics. Closer to home, in 1992 the presidency of the United States passed from the Republican party—Aiken's party—to the Democratic party, and several realignments of domestic and international policies have taken place partly as a result and partly in spite of this change.

These changes and continuities may require that we think differently about Aiken's career and its potential lessons about American politics and diplomacy at the end of the twentieth century. There is no doubt, however, that there is an "Aiken legacy": George Aiken the man, George Aiken the politician, and George Aiken the statesman do continue to offer us lessons and models for the conduct of public life. It is for that reason that scholars, friends, students, and colleagues gathered in 1991 to hear about and discuss Aiken's career in the U.S. Senate. And it is for that reason that we have thought it worthwhile to present to a wider public these reflections on the Aiken legacy.

George D. Aiken while governor of Vermont, 1937–1941. Courtesy of Bailey/Howe Library, University of Vermont.

1

Growing Up Progressive

James Wright

*I*N ONE OF HIS ORAL HISTORY SESSIONS WITH Charles Morrissey shortly after he retired from the U.S. Senate, George Aiken spoke about Winston Churchill, the novelist from Cornish, New Hampshire, whose books were immensely popular in the first decade of the twentieth century. Churchill was an intriguing man who played a pivotal role in organizing the Republican reform movement in the Granite State. Aiken told Morrissey that Churchill's novel *Coniston*, published in 1906, was one of his "favorite books." He recalled *Coniston* as describing how the Boston and Maine Railroad "ran the State of New Hampshire."[1]

The senator spoke of *Coniston* and Churchill often and allowed that they had had some impact on the development of his political ideas. Because of my own work on progressivism in New Hampshire and because of Churchill's major role in this movement, I found these connections to Aiken intriguing. My essay examines what it was like to grow up in the Connecticut

River valley during the Progressive period, which, for our purposes, can be dated generally as the first fifteen years or so of the twentieth century.

Any student of New England politics is fascinated by the differences between New Hampshire and Vermont. Certainly some of these differences have come about because New Hampshire has been more urban, more industrial, and more ethnically heterogeneous than Vermont since the middle of the nineteenth century. And the political conflicts that relate to these characteristics have been imbued with a particular quality, even at times pungency, in New Hampshire. It is important to note as well that the two states have experienced similar historical forces that have fundamentally altered and shaped their economic and political institutions: the Civil War, the process of adaptation and finally decline of most traditional forms of agriculture, the growth of the tourist business and the recreation industry, the influence of Boston's economic institutions, and the continuing erosion of the traditionally insular small-town culture. Each state has been dominated by the Republican party for much of the post–Civil War period, but it is a Republican party that was altered by the consequences of national political phenomena: progressivism, the depression and New Deal, Barry Goldwater's 1964 presidential campaign, and the rise of the Sun Belt. The river separating the states isn't really that wide.

In his Senate diary on January 1, 1972, George Aiken reflected, "Looking off to the east we can see a twenty-mile stretch of the New Hampshire hills east of the Connecticut River. Mount Monadnock dominates the view now that the leaves are off the trees. On clear nights the lights of New Hampshire homes blink at us from the distance, while during late summer and early fall mornings we look out from our vantage point of fourteen hundred feet elevation in full sunshine over a sea of fog filling the Connecticut Valley."[2] Progressivism did begin to blink early from the New Hampshire hills. And perhaps not coincidentally, the area around Mount Monadnock was an important center for this reform movement.

It seems likely that Senator Aiken used *Coniston* as a generic title referring to all of Churchill's political novels. *Coniston* was the story of the erosion of the old hill country political machines in the mid-nineteenth century. Churchill's protagonist in this story was Jethro Bass (a character most critics believe was modeled closely after New Hampshire's controversial Republican leader Ruel Durkee, 1807–1885). Through judicious cultivation of rural constituents and of other members of the New Hampshire legislature, Bass was the real power broker in Churchill's rural political kingdom. The novel ends with Bass recognizing that his days are over and that the lawyers, representing the railroad, will provide the new political leadership.[3] Because this story has no clear moral resolution, I am confident that Senator Aiken enjoyed it as a piece of fiction but did not necessarily find in it the political blueprint that he later suggested he did. It is important to note, however, that I may be in the minority in this view, for no less a figure than Churchill himself described *Coniston* as representing his political platform. If so, it was a platform of moral condemnation rather than one that articulated a vision or a program.

The more likely candidate for Senator Aiken's blueprint and the more logical exposition of Churchill's platform was Churchill's sequel to *Coniston,* the novel *Mr. Crewe's Career*.[4] Set in the early twentieth century, this novel described the railroad and its tremendous political power in Concord. Mr. Crewe, Humphrey Crewe, was a dilettante politician, a gentleman indifferent to politics and indeed to most affairs of the world until he and his friends, political neophytes all, joined in a campaign of moral outrage to challenge the railroad and its lobby. This story, representing as it does the flowering of reform, probably had the greatest influence on young George Aiken. Published in 1908, when Aiken was sixteen years old, the story of Mr. Crewe and of the forces of moral reform that he led became one of the most popular books of the period.

Mr. Crewe's Career was dedicated "to the men who in every State in the Union are engaged in the struggle for purer politics." If Crewe, the naive but idealistic and energetic reformer, was frustrated in his effort to secure his party's gubernatorial nomination because the machine, in a state of panic, had finally stopped him at a riotous convention, the book nonetheless ended on an upbeat tone. It was clear that by flexing power too freely, the old machine —the railroad forces—had spelled its own destruction. As Churchill had warned in *Coniston*, the end of the rural boss was at best a mixed blessing: "after the Boss came along certain Things without souls." In the sequel to the novel, these soulless things met their match in an outraged citizenry that would reclaim government for the people.

In 1893, when George Aiken was an infant, President Grover Cleveland remarked, "The lessons of paternalism ought to be unlearned and the better lesson taught that while the people should patriotically and cheerfully support their Government, its functions do not include the support of the people."[5] Seventeen years later, in his New Nationalism speech, Theodore Roosevelt said, quite simply, that "the object of government is the welfare of the people."[6]

These were more than individual differences in political rhetoric, partisan values, or even personal political philosophy. Roosevelt's sentiments reflected a fundamental alteration in the parameters of political debate and in the understanding of the limits of governmental concern and influence. Aiken's childhood coincided with this process of redefinition and change. And the Progressives of northern New England, the Progressives of Vermont and New Hampshire, shared fully in this process. If they moved against Churchill's "Things without souls," they did so by putting some soul into government.

New Hampshire progressivism was first and foremost a political movement that aimed at reducing the economic power and political influence of the Boston and Maine Railroad. There was by the early twentieth century a widespread perception that the Boston and Maine ran the government of New Hampshire.[7] If the description exaggerated, it did not significantly distort the tremendous influence that the railroad, operating within the Republican party, had over the state government. It was certainly impossible even to secure consideration of legislation that could have negative consequences for the Boston and Maine corporation.

If power does not necessarily beget corruption, it often begets arrogance. And it was this, as much as anything, that led to the downfall of the Boston and Maine's political machine and the concomitant rise of Progressive reform. Granite Staters seemed to tolerate the railroad's wink-and-nod influence over taxes, railroad regulations, and legislative and gubernatorial nominations—those things that protected and enhanced the Boston and Maine's position. But when chief railroad operative Frank Streeter, a Concord lawyer, also used the railroad's political machine to replace a Prohibition law with a more liberal local-option approach to liquor regulation and when he supported a legislative charter for the New England Breeder's Club, he elicited anger and outrage. The Breeder's Club, an innocuous-appearing organization dedicated to improving horse stock in New Hampshire, was in fact a corporation owned by New York and Saratoga interests that operated a racetrack at Salem, New Hampshire. Their charter even permitted wagering at their track, a remarkable exception to New Hampshire's tough antigambling law.

These actions triggered a significant set of reactions from a powerful coalition of offended citizens. The sudden legalization of liquor and gambling permits was enough to move many of the state's religious leaders to action and to mobilize the broader forces of reform. Dartmouth president William Jewett Tucker assumed an important public role in lashing out at the railroad forces. This was a complicated and difficult thing for Tucker to do because several powerful members of his board of trustees, including Streeter, were involved with the railroad. Nonetheless, Tucker, the last of Dartmouth's minister presidents, spoke out at a mass rally in Manchester at which he insisted upon "an aroused public sentiment." Tucker believed that New Hampshire had been humiliated. He insisted, "Let the sense of humiliation remain upon us until we have taken measures sufficient to recover the honor of the State."8

Just as outrage and recovering honor were components of the Progressive reform movement, so were more practical political objectives. Many of the Granite State's young political leaders had felt restrained by the railroad's political operatives. Calling themselves the Lincoln Republicans, they formed a coalition within the Republican party in 1906. These reformers tried to invoke the idealistic roots of their party. Attempting to thwart railroad's automatic slotting of a gubernatorial candidate, they used the state's caucus and convention system to field a candidate of their own: Winston Churchill.

Because of the popularity of his novels, Churchill was likely New Hampshire's most widely known citizen. He had moved to Cornish in 1899, helped to form the highly visible summer colony there, and made his home a meeting place for artists, writers, and public figures. The novelist enjoyed discussions and tennis games with young Herbert Croly, whose book *The New Nationalism* was an important statement of reform. President Theodore Roosevelt visited Churchill's home in 1902, and the two became friends and regular correspondents.[9]

Churchill became involved in state politics in 1902 when he successfully ran as a Republican candidate for the state legislature. It seemed a bit of a lark, for Churchill had no clear political agenda or policy objective. By 1906 he certainly had not established himself as a reformer. Yet in many ways he was an obvious choice for the antirailroad forces to support: he was well known, financially secure, and sufficiently independent so that the railroad operatives could not take any punitive action against him.

The 1906 Lincoln Republican movement was essentially defensive and regenerative, with no clear reform program. In a chaotic state convention (which became the setting for Mr. Crewe's defeat in the novel), Churchill and the Lincoln Republicans lost the nomination through some machine maneuvers that were controversial at best. But the Lincoln Republican movement became the basis for an ongoing reform impetus in New Hampshire. The railroad would never again control the state unchallenged. In the legislative sessions of 1907 and 1909, a reform coalition successfully challenged the old guard leadership on several occasions. And in 1910 the Progressive Republicans, utilizing the state's first direct primary election, secured the gubernatorial nomination for Churchill's ally, Robert Perkins Bass of Peterborough. Bass won the general election and earned a national reputation as a reform governor. Despite the ironic coincidence in surnames, Robert Bass bore no relationship or resemblance to the fictional Jethro Bass.

Robert Bass's family had moved back to their ancestral New Hampshire home in the 1880s after amassing a comfortable fortune in Chicago. A friend and admirer of Theodore Roosevelt, Robert Bass led his Reform Republicans in 1910 with a much broader agenda than simply taking back control of the state. He pursued this agenda vigorously during the 1911 legislative session. And from the first flurry of Lincoln Republican reform to the beginning of World War I, much of New Hampshire law was rewritten. Regulation of lobbying activities and direct primary legislation effectively throttled railroad political influence, and the Public Service Commission restrained its economic power. Insurance and banking regulations, new public health and welfare laws, new employment regulations and labor relations requirements, a new juvenile court system, health and safety regulations and restrictions, workmen's compensation laws and regulation of child labor, significant conservation legislation (including a comprehensive forest protection law), fundamental changes in support of education, regulation of automobiles and the development of a state highway system, new government budgeting procedures, and fundamental changes in the state tax codes—all represented a basic alteration in the nature of New Hampshire government.

Roosevelt's magazine, *The Outlook*, described New Hampshire as "well to the front among Republican progressive states."[10] It was. But the forces that contributed to reform victory also led to defeat. The Progressives in New Hampshire split badly over Roosevelt's insurgency Bull Moose campaign for the presidency in 1912. Bass and Churchill led a bolt from their party in order to stand at Armageddon with Roosevelt against the incumbent Republican, William Howard Taft. The Progressive majority in

New Hampshire, always tenuous, never recovered from that bloodletting.

Vermont followed many of the same processes of reform during this period. Under governors Fletcher Proctor (1906–1908) and Allen Fletcher (1912–1915), Vermont, too, established commissions to regulate the state's railroad and utilities and initiated workmen's compensation, protection and conservation of Vermont's forests and natural resources, and a direct primary system that was finally implemented in 1916.[11] If Vermont's Progressive era reforms were somewhat less comprehensive than those of New Hampshire, they were also accompanied by far less Republican warfare. U.S. senator Ernest Gibson Jr. supported Roosevelt, but his backing did not lead to the temporary destruction of his party in Vermont in the way that Robert Bass's and Winston Churchill's support did in New Hampshire. Vermonters tend to go about their business more quietly than Granite Staters.

The historian of Vermont progressivism, Winston Allen Flint, believed that Vermont represented at bottom a reform echo of national progressivism. Obviously, there is some truth to this, for, in the twentieth century at least, no state in the American political system can be free from the forces that are unleashed elsewhere in the Union. And Hiram Johnson in California, Robert LaFollette in Wisconsin, Charles Evans Hughes in New York, Woodrow Wilson in New Jersey, Theodore Roosevelt and Woodrow Wilson in the White House, as well as Robert Bass and Winston Churchill in New Hampshire combined with thousands of others to conduct a national Progressive symphony that surely found ready ears and resonance in Vermont. But Green Mountain progressivism had its own integrity, its own character, its own agenda, and its own consequence.

So George Aiken did grow up a Progressive. And we can only accept his own judgment that the exciting novels of Winston Churchill, as well as the real-life drama of New Hampshire politics that they mirrored, helped shape his sense of limit and possibility, his understanding of political propriety, his appreciation of the appropriate and necessary role of government in the twentieth century—*helped* shape. For growing up Progressive surely involved more than this to a Vermonter such as Aiken; it involved more than lights blinking off of Mount Monadnock.

Roosevelt was the first president whom Aiken recalled seeing. As he later wrote, "One of the great regrets of my life is that I was not old enough to vote for him in 1912 but how I did holler."[12] Aiken recalled his father's support for Roosevelt: "Teddy Roosevelt was a rebel and I think my father had it in his blood somewhat. And it had come down from generation to generation." Of his own decision to run for the Vermont state legislature in 1922, Aiken simply said, "It ran in the family, I think…. In each generation all the way back to the 1770's there had been some member of my family in the legislature…. So I guess it could have been in the blood."[13]

Growing up Progressive may not have been as natural and biological an evolution as Aiken thought, but the process and the product were nonetheless shaped by a homegrown Vermont environment. The Vermont Republican party had its origins in reform, and the Progressive movement reaffirmed this past as much as it invented or imported something new and different. The Vermont Republican party's resilience during the New Deal years, a resilience characterized by Aiken, represented the skillful maneuver of a party that managed to add to several of the Democratic reforms while still maintaining its own integrity and identity.[14] Governor Aiken's open letter to the Republican National Committee in 1937 was an articulate and positive challenge to his Grand Old Party to reform its processes and recognize its public obligations. The party had been devastated in the 1936 presidential elections, Governor Alf Landon of Kansas carrying only Maine and Vermont against Franklin Roosevelt. Aiken said that Vermonters' support could not be assumed in the future: "to purge the Party organization of its reactionary and unfair elements, to focus its forces on the recognition of the youth of our nation, to prepare immediately an affirmative program—that is the demand which the Republican leadership of Vermont makes on the Republican leadership of the nation."[15] Among the young New

Hampshire politicians who were inspired by the Progressive reform movement in his state was Charles Tobey.[16] He was a protégé of Robert Bass, and his political career had some similarities to that of Aiken. Aiken and Tobey represented the Progressive wing of Yankee republicanism; as governors they managed to respond to the depression without succumbing to the New Deal.

In June 1950 six U.S. senators joined with Senator Margaret Chase Smith of Maine to sponsor her "Declaration of Conscience." More than forty-one years later, the statement reads like a moderate, even unremarkable document. The declaration noted, "Those of us who shout the loudest about Americanism … are all too frequently those, who by our own words and acts, ignore some of the basic principles of Americanism." These principles were defined as "the right to criticize; the right to hold unpopular beliefs; the right to protest; and the right of independent thought." Among Senator Smith's cosponsors were two other northern New England senators—two other Yankee Republicans: Senator Charles Tobey of New Hampshire and Senator George Aiken of Vermont.[17]

The "Declaration of Conscience" was the first statement made in the U.S. Senate critical of the junior senator from Wisconsin. The cosigners of this document would continue for the next several years to express their concern about Joseph McCarthy and in 1954 would participate in the Senate Resolution of Censure that finally marked McCarthy's political downfall. This vote was difficult for Republicans, but as Senator Aiken recalled, "I finally had to vote to censure Joe. I didn't want to, but had to."[18]

I guess it is the imperative as much as the action that I find intriguing. And I would hypothesize that growing up Progressive may have played some role in shaping the imperative. It was not an automatic conditioned response, however, for Tobey's Senate colleague Styles Bridges, who became a strong supporter of McCarthy and conservative economic causes, had also grown up Progressive.

George Aiken did indeed represent what may be a dying political force outside of Vermont, and perhaps even a less influential force within Vermont: a tradition of moderate, responsive,

Progressive Yankee republicanism. The dramatic New Hampshire battles for reform early in the twentieth century, fictional as well as real, likely had a shaping influence on Aiken's politics, as he suggested in his comments late in life, when his political career had ended. But so did family and neighbors and the traditions of Vermont politics generally and Vermont republicanism specifically. Governor Aiken wrote in 1938 that Vermont had "a heritage of ideals" and that these included "principles of loving liberty, of self-reliance, of thrift and of liberalism," all of which have left Vermonters with an important sense of self-respect.[19] It was a quiet Progressive heritage in which he grew up. But it was also a Progressive heritage that he solidified, advanced, and finally bequeathed to his party, his state, and his country.

Aiken and Senator Margaret Chase Smith of Maine at the Republican National Convention, San Francisco, July 1964. Courtesy of Bailey/Howe Library, University of Vermont.

2

George Aiken: A Republican Senator and His Party

Herbert S. Parmet

*M*Y LAST ENCOUNTER WITH GEORGE AIKEN WAS accidental—and quite anonymous. I remember it as one recalls all moments filled with points of reference. Richard Nixon had just been sworn in for a second term as president of the United States. Watergate was only on the verge of realizing its potential as an issue. After some vigorous devastation from the air, combined with equally strong pounding on the will of President Nguyen Van Thieu of South Vietnam, the United States was finally extricating itself from Southeast Asia. The Nixon administration, at that high point, decided to take on the Democratic Congress by impounding funds earmarked for domestic programs.

I stood at the elevator bank of the Russell Senate Office Building when, within that crowd on the move, out stepped George Aiken. He looked gray and craggy and maintained his unsmiling, no-nonsense stride, perfectly in keeping with the "conscience of the Senate." There was, I remember thinking, something anomalous about his aura of integrity amidst the collapse of confidence on Capitol Hill. His reputation for honesty was as secure as Nixon's was for venality.

George Aiken was a good, decent, kindly man, maybe even the most civilized of men. He could breathe and appreciate life around his native Putney. He could, as he did, tell historian Charles Morrissey that progressivism came naturally to him. Hadn't he spent a lifetime absorbing the freedom of his Vermont woods instead of being imprisoned by forty-story buildings? That kind of artificial, modern-world ambience was the ultimate corruption of the Garden. In tones reminiscent of Henry David Thoreau, Aiken said that "out in the woods you can think better."

In some way he also harked back to a nonpartisan tradition of the early-twentieth-century Progressives, one that long predates the lament of political scientists since the 1970s about the demise of parties. We have heard much about George Aiken the Vermonter. In his own time, of course, he was far from alone in branding the New Deal tyrannical. Yet even then he was notable for taking the long-range view. He warned the Republican National Committee to "accept in general the social aims which the opposing party has the wisdom to adopt," and he called for an end to the "hate Roosevelt" campaign.[1]

Aiken was one of the last Bull Moosers. His father served as a long-term Bull Mooser in the Vermont legislature. As one of the state's most progressive governors, Aiken continued his fight, begun as a first-term representative from Putney, with the private power company interests that had been gouging users with the highest rates in the country. As he told interviewer Gregory Sanford, he was opposed not only by the power companies but also by "the railroads, ... the granite industry and the marble industry, even the insurance [industry]—the big boys."[2] He could, for good measure, have thrown in the banks among his enemies.

In 1961 *Burlington Free Press* columnist Franklin B. Smith wrote that Aiken and other "pseudo-Republicans" should form their own "political party and have the courage to call it the semi-socialist party."[3] Little wonder that part of the George Aiken legacy was the founding of a moderate Young Republican movement in the state.[4] What this should underscore is that, for all his maverick tendencies, George Aiken was a loyal party man. Under Dwight Eisenhower, for example, when Joseph McCarthy was doing his utmost to discredit the integrity of the U.S. Senate, Aiken took action in 1954 that was less flamboyant than the famous floor remarks made by his colleague, Ralph Flanders; but in terms of his own committee seniority, it was far more costly. Faced with the threat of McCarthy's grabbing a vacancy on the Foreign Relations Committee, Aiken blocked that move by surrendering his own thirteen years of seniority on the Senate Labor and Public Welfare Committee to claim the Foreign Relations seat.[5]

Even so, he stood with his party. A few weeks before the Senate vote on the resolution to condemn McCarthy, he commented on his "reluctance" to take a stand on the censure motion. His rationale for silence was simple: "it is impossible to tell the exact form of the resolution on which the Senate may finally be asked to vote."[6] When the vote on the resolution introduced by Arthur Watkins of Utah did come on December 2, Aiken joined that half of his party—Republicans split evenly—that voted to censure McCarthy.

Aiken was most at home and most visible on the national scene during the Eisenhower years, when the Republicans controlled Congress. His actions were reminiscent of his earlier participation with so-called Young Turks in opposition to Robert A. Taft's Senate leadership. He had, in fact, been one of those who signed Margaret Chase Smith's "Declaration of Conscience" in 1950, which is often regarded as the first condemnation of McCarthy's assault on civil liberties. Under Eisenhower, especially during the period of conservative senator Barry Goldwater's ascendancy in the administration's later years, Aiken helped lead the attack against the old guard. But the style of George Aiken and his allies was no match for an administration that insisted on placating the Right, and, without presidential support, the moderate wing of the party was incapable of exercising leadership.[7] Still, Aiken the critic remained alive, chiding the weekly "Ev and

Charlie show"—as the joint news conferences held by Senator Everett Dirksen (R–Ill.) and Representative Charles Halleck (R–Ind.) came to be called—for perpetuating a "status quo" image of the party.[8]

Historians usually characterize the Eisenhower presidency as incompetent, inert, and neglectful; as holding the line or sitting on a volcano; or as making substantive tactical gains by means of an invisible hand. The composite view, however, states the problem: nobody could credit the general in the White House with shaping the Republican party into whatever image he found suitable. On the contrary, his failure to support William Scranton's challenge to Barry Goldwater for the 1964 Republican presidential nomination showed that Eisenhower was not willing or able to be a conciliator recasting the party in his own image.

Reshaping the Republican party as a moderate or progressive force in U.S. politics was left to the amateurs. I speak here of the long-forgotten Ripon Society, that group of Republican intellectuals—"elitists" to some—who adopted their name from party history to attempt what they termed a much-needed "bridging of the gulf that has separated much of the GOP from the intellectual and political community for the past fifty years." As Nicol Rae put it, they "hoped to attract the young, professional middle class"— their so-called frontlash constituency—to the Republican party and thereby the backlash of northern blue-collar and southern rural white voters. Viewing themselves as progressive (and therefore, naturally, enlightened), the Ripon Society wrote that the party had to move in their direction, not toward the "forgotten Americans" or "silent majority" in order to

> win the confidence of the "New Americans," who are not at home in the politics of another generation: the new middle classes of the suburbs of the North and West—who have left the Democratic cities but have not yet found a home in the Republican party ... who represent the hope for peaceful racial adjustment and who are insulted by a racist appeal more fitting another generation.

The Riponites summarized the importance of winning these "New Americans" by saying, "These and others like them hold the key to the future of our politics."9 The Ripon Society entered the 1968 election year, however, with an annual budget of only $95,000. By contrast, the rightist Young Americans for Freedom commanded $25,000 per month.

Although the Riponites made themselves felt during the Nixon administration, Republican power remained, and prevailed, among those with conservative ideologies backed by money and conservative political bases. The Riponites were, moreover, handicapped by looking for leadership to an "inherently loose and heterogeneous group" of Republican governors.10 Another group, the Council of Republican Organizations, did no better, and neither did the so-called Republicans for Progress led by Charles P. Taft, a brother of Robert A. Taft and ex-mayor of Cincinnati. As Rae wisely pointed out, in words applicable to the career of George Aiken, these centrist Republicans were liberals who "still placed their trust in personality and old-style party-elite politics rather than grass roots organization."11 Little wonder that during this period between the Goldwater rebellion and the Reagan coup, a Vermont paper, the *Rutland Herald*, observed in 1965, "With the right wing firmly in control of the Young Republican organization and their elders prominent in the Legislature, Vermonters may be inclined to wonder what has happened to the Republican Party which Senator George D. Aiken was talking about ... with its progressive legislative traditions."12

Aiken explained that his only reason for going to the San Francisco Republican National Convention in 1964 was to place Margaret Chase Smith's name in nomination for president. He acknowledged that he did not go along with his state's delegation to make the Goldwater nomination unanimous. For months before going to California, he held out against committing himself for Goldwater; he resisted pleas of fellow Vermonters that the Arizonan was needed to fight against communism and for fiscal integrity. Goldwater's request for Aiken's support, as early as January 1964, drew a simple suggestion to debate the specifics.

Aiken asked that issues and not personality determine the outcome as a way to achieve unification before election day.[13]

Republican moderates virtually abdicated their opportunities after 1964. In effect, they emulated Eisenhower by opening the field to the party's right wing, and the party has continued to drift in that direction ever since, with the Goldwater electoral disaster and Johnson's legislative successes mere pauses in the rightist drive. Aiken, moreover, remained at bottom the good Republican; he kept his partisan credentials. In 1966, for example, just before that year's turnabout congressional election, he confided to a constituent and old friend his thought that Johnson's Great Society was making the country "more socialistic every day."[14]

Nixon's return from the electoral dead was the next major test of the GOP center. Again, the party succumbed to several factors pushing it to the right. One was Nixon's role as the titular leader of the party after the electorate's repudiation of Goldwater. The Riponites stood virtually alone in holding out for Eisenhower's "modern Republicanism." John Lindsay of New York, George Romney of Michigan, and other liberals, however, mismanaged their campaigns and destroyed their chances to serve as potential leaders. Nixon also barnstormed harder than any other Republican, especially during the congressional elections of 1966. Moreover, a social and economic backlash that gathered strength throughout the decade coalesced into what conservative commentator Kevin Phillips called the "emerging Republican majority." Nixon's resurrection, therefore, seems less surprising in retrospect, a case of the country's moving toward him as much as he to the country. It was, according to Rae, "the final triumph of a strategy of conciliation vis-à-vis the Republican right over the ideological-adversarial approach favored by the liberal intellectuals of the Ripon Society."[15]

In a last-minute effort to recapture the middle road just before Nixon's presidential nomination in summer 1968, Aiken declared that Nelson Rockefeller, governor of New York and the centrist challenge to Goldwater in 1964, would be the best vote-getter in the East.[16] But Aiken's light went out as Nixon's came back on. In his final days in Washington, the senator was perceived as a Nixon man. In fact, he and Nixon had shared much congeniality during the 1950s: Nixon understood farmers better than did Eisenhower. Nixon, according to Aiken, was "well to the left of the present Administration" generally and on agricultural matters, "but not so far to the left as some would want him to be." Both men opposed the so-called right-to-work laws, and Aiken thought of Nixon as an enemy of the party's reactionaries.[17] Ultimately, the two men went together. Nothing illustrates that better than the two final crises of Aiken's and Nixon's careers: Vietnam and Watergate.

The Vietnam experience best illustrated the tragic failure of all moderates. With their middle ground undercut almost daily, with simultaneous calls for accelerated escalation and abrupt withdrawal, they temporized with little effect. As a member of the Senate Foreign Relations Committee, Aiken, together with almost everyone else in the Senate, voted to give President Johnson his Tonkin Gulf resolution. In early 1965, just before the North Vietnamese attack on the base at Pleiku, Aiken was invited to the White House as part of a group of key congressional figures. They heard the president explain that Operation Rolling Thunder was about to start. "I protested rather vehemently," Aiken recalled six years later, "stating that those people would react the same way we would, but President Johnson's advisors had apparently convinced him that it was a way to bring the war to an early and satisfactory conclusion."[18]

When Aiken subsequently traveled to Vietnam on a Foreign Relations Committee fact-finding mission, he helped produce a report that was openly pessimistic. "We made a huge military commitment to that part of the world," he said in 1968, "simply because we did not have the wit, the imagination, or the courage to devise a political strategy to suit a political problem."[19]

But George Aiken was not about to be cornered. In a Senate speech that same spring, he said that the bombing, even if necessary, was "profoundly distasteful" to many Americans, and he made plain that he was disturbed that the military action was being undertaken without appropriate consultation with Congress.[20] On October 19, 1966, Aiken told the Senate that the way to a political solution was for the United States to declare that the military objectives in Vietnam had been met and look for ways to end the fighting. Still, he continued to take a middle ground. He cosponsored both the Cooper-Church and Mansfield amendments, designed to set withdrawal dates for U.S. troops, and he went along with other bills aimed at limiting the conflict. He nevertheless balked at cutting the defense budget or joining with Gaylord Nelson (D–Wis.) and Charles Goodell (R–N.Y.) in their attempt to prohibit the use of defoliant chemicals. By spring 1972, Aiken was in the headlines as a supporter of Nixon's plan to bomb Hanoi and Haiphong and mine Haiphong harbor.

A Ralph Nader Senate project report that year quoted "many observers" who felt that "the veteran dove had turned hawk, a suspicious about-face in an important political year."[21] But Aiken argued that the situation had changed, not his outlook. North Vietnam was clearly the aggressor, obviously supplied with "invasion weapons, mostly from Russia, whereas our supplies sent to the South Vietnamese troops have consisted primarily of defense weapons. I believe that Hanoi committed a serious error and if, as is reported, Russia has been egging them on, then the Soviets are only creating more difficulties for themselves."[22] To some Vermonters in spring 1972, he appeared defensive:

> Don't get the idea that I have changed my mind or support all actions taken in Indo-China by the last three Presidents. What I want to know is—Are the American people willing to support now an acceptance of the North Vietnamese terms? Personally, I think that the slaughter which would take place in South Vietnam would be several times greater than that which occurred in Bangladesh several months ago.[23]

The second and final crisis of this period was Watergate. Aiken made a revealing comment in his Senate diary for March 31, 1973, when Nixon had pulled the United States out of Vietnam but the Watergate charges were heating up: "he isn't worried too much about the success of the party, or the lack of it, after he leaves office." Nine weeks later, he regretted the low state of the president's standing because, as he added, "there are so many things to his credit, so many things that have been good for the people of the whole world."24 When Godfrey Sperling Jr. of the *Christian Science Monitor* solicited Aiken's views on Nixon and Watergate, the senator's loyalty to the president held fast. He replied that the president should neither be impeached nor should he resign.25 Nothing, however, upset anti-administration Vermonters as much as Aiken's association with the Nixon "Saturday night massacre," when he defended the president's order to fire special Watergate prosecutor Archibald Cox. That, more than anything else, encouraged Vermonters' beliefs that their senator's tenure had been overextended.26 Aiken only confirmed their suspicions on November 14, 1973, when he urged Congress "either [to] impeach him or get off his back."27 Aiken was present with a small group in the White House on August 8, 1974, to hear the president explain why he intended to resign the next day. In his diary entry Aiken recalled the scene: "it was an extremely sorry and emotional occasion with many tears being shed, including those of the President himself, who had difficulty in starting his story to us, and finally left the Cabinet Room in a highly emotional and tearful condition."28 By that point, few should have been surprised when Aiken endorsed Gerald Ford's pardon of the former president.

In 1974, at the age of eighty-two, George Aiken decided against running again for the Senate. He would clearly have been reelected, despite all the doubts raised by his position on Vietnam and his support of Nixon throughout Watergate. One survey, conducted in the state by Market Opinion Research, showed that 77 percent of Vermonters still expressed a great deal of confidence in their senior senator.29 Aiken had long since been hailed as the "dean of all Senate Republicans"; as Stephen Hess and David Broder once noted, "He never asserts himself, but other Senators often come to him."30 But as two Washington political observers put it, "the delights of the capital remained resistible" to the former Putney farmer.31

The Reagan presidency gave us an unexpected lesson for Aiken's Senate career, especially in the president's ability to lead with a firm set of convictions. Whatever else may be written about Reagan, this will constitute an important, and positive, characteristic—his doing, in other words, exactly what moderate Republicans failed to do. As Rae noted in her study of the demise of liberal republicanism, "Liberal Republican candidates continued to place electoral appeals in terms of personality or electability, rather than of political principle, frequently acknowledging the validity of most of the right's doctrines, while arguing that they would have to be modified to win votes for the party."[32] Fear of rightists intimidated Nelson Rockefeller and George Romney from their own vigorous counterattack after the Goldwater debacle. The Eisenhower wing settled on a Republican stalwart, Ray Bliss, to lead the party's national committee, in the hope that a good broker might do the job of keeping the rightists in check. We know how it all wound up by 1968.

True Reaganites faulted President George Bush for ideological impurities. In effect, he looked the other way after Tiananmen Square, he raised taxes, he reduced nuclear arms, and his "new world order" offended the right-wing isolationists represented by Patrick Buchanan. Still, all this seems weird. We watched Bush bury a Democratic Congress under forty-six vetoes, a new record. Nonetheless, political analyst William Schneider, writing in the *National Journal* in October 1991, suggested that his survival and apparent popular approval up to that date, despite domestic failures, can be attributed in large part to the popular tendency to blame the Congress rather than the president.[33]

The George Aikens of our political world are worthy of monuments; they are indeed men of conscience, right or wrong. The rest of us, however, left without a viable opposition, may be left without the luxury of choice. We are, in effect, trapped in a narrow ideological spectrum that inhibits the emergence of a constructive dialogue. I am confident Aiken would have agreed with that assessment of the current problem in our political institutions. But this is the trouble with such men of goodwill: could he have worked to do something about it? Would he have wanted to?

Mike Mansfield and Aiken at their daily breakfast meeting, Senate cafeteria, 1970. Courtesy of Bailey/Howe Library, University of Vermont.

3

The U.S. Senate in the Era of George Aiken, 1941–1975

Donald A. Ritchie

*A*T THE END OF THE SECOND WEEK OF JANUARY 1974, Senator George Aiken recorded in his diary that he had celebrated his thirty-third anniversary of taking the oath of office as a senator. Writing a month after Gerald Ford had become the nation's first appointed vice president, Aiken recalled that he had been sworn in as a senator by Vice President John Nance Garner in 1941. The only incident he could remember from his first day was that on his way from Vermont to Washington, one of his staff members, Lola Pierotti, had lost her hatbox at the Newark airport and an aide had run halfway across the field to retrieve it. Just a month after writing that entry, in February 1974, Senator Aiken announced that he would not stand again for reelection, even though polls showed he could have won by as much as 70 percent of the vote.[1]

Enormous changes occurred in the United States during Aiken's three decades as a senator, which covered the period from

Pearl Harbor to the Watergate scandal; much also changed in the U.S. Senate. In this chapter, taking as my time frame the parameters of Aiken's career in Washington and citing Aiken's own sage observations, I discuss some of the significant institutional and structural transformations of the Senate in the era of George Aiken.

The Senate that greeted George Aiken in 1941 was considerably different from the one he left in 1975. In fact, it had changed more during those years than during any other period in its two-hundred-year history. When he arrived there were ninety-six senators representing forty-eight states. Those ninety-six senators had an average of six staff members apiece, or about 600 combined, and there were another 200 staff for its forty-five standing and special committees. The legislative branch appropriation stood at less than $50 million. By the time Aiken left, the number of senators had increased to 100 and they represented fifty states. In contrast to this modest growth, the size of senators' staffs had passed 3,000, with another 1,000 committee staff members serving just twenty-three standing and special committees. The legislative appropriations reached $552 million by 1974. And those figures seem modest when compared to statistics today.2

Of course, not everyone's staff grew so precipitously. According to the *Congressional Staff Directory*, there were six staff members in Senator Aiken's office in 1941, and when he retired thirty-four years later, there were ten—counting Lola, his administrative assistant, whom the senator had taken off the payroll when he married her in 1967. The Senate staff began to grow in earnest with the Legislative Reorganization Act of 1946. Following the vast increase in federal activity during the New Deal and World War II and responding in part to the reorganization of the executive branch in the late 1930s, Congress moved to streamline and modernize its operations. The lack of a professional staff had made Congress increasingly dependent upon executive branch agencies and corporate lobbyists to prepare legislation and even to draft reports and speeches. A proliferation of committees, many of which had outlived their usefulness, also consumed a great deal of senators' time. During the war there had been complaints that some military officials spent more time testifying before congressional committees than planning strategy. At the end of the war, Congress appointed a joint committee to examine the problem. Under the able leadership of Senator Robert La Follette Jr. (R and Progressive–Wis.) and Representative Mike Monroney (D–Okla.), and with political scientist George Galloway as staff director, a comprehensive reform program reduced the number of committees and created the Senate's first professional staff structure.[3]

In an oral history interview with the Senate Historical Office, Francis Wilcox described the staff of the Senate Foreign Relations Committee at the end of the war:

> We had a clerk, Bob Shirley, who taught at the University of Maryland half-time. He was the chief clerk. We had an assistant clerk, Emmett O'Grady, who could take dictation and type, run a stenotype machine, and take care of the office generally. And we had a secretary from Senator Connally's [the chairman] office, who devoted half her time to the committee. That was the staff of the Foreign Relations Committee. Now, you can see, at that point there could be no adversary relationship between the two branches of the government, because most of the professional work clearly had to be done in the State Department.... Speeches had to be written there; committee reports to the Senate were prepared by the executive branch; there was no mechanism really by which the Senate could act independently.... You can see that with a staff of only three—two-and-a-half people—the Senate committee could not function very effectively.[4]

As a result of the Legislative Reorganization Act, Wilcox became the first chief of staff of the Senate Foreign Relations Committee and proceeded to build a nonpartisan professional staff. It was small at first, just a few foreign policy specialists who worked for both Democratic and Republican senators. Quite often the same staff member would be asked to draft reports and speeches for both the majority and minority. One staff member, Pat Holt, recalled how once during the early 1960s he had handled the staff work for an international coffee agreement. Republican Senator Karl Mundt (R–S. Dak.) came to Holt and said he wanted to speak to the minority man on the issue. Holt said there wasn't one. "Well, I want to oppose the coffee agreement, and where can I get some help?" the senator asked. "From me," Holt replied and gave him the case against the treaty and drafted his speech opposing it. Mundt later told the staff director that he was very satisfied, much to his surprise.[5]

The initial concept was that the nonpartisan, professional staff would work for the committee as a whole, and that any member could call upon it for anything relating to committee business. Staff members were supposed to keep a low profile. When drawing up their regulations, the committee dipped back into some FDR-era language and wrote that the staff should have a "passion for anonymity." Senator Aiken, however, protested ("Let's leave the passion out of this"), and the phrase was dropped. But the staff was specifically prohibited from publishing or speaking out on an issue without the permission of the chairman or the chief of staff.[6]

Over time the small professional staff of the committee grew in size and power, which caused some discomfort for Senator Aiken. In February 1972 he recorded in his diary: "Some members of the [Foreign Relations] committee staff are getting pretty high-handed, and, like some members of other Senate committees, they seem to feel that they rather than the elected members of the Senate should determine policies." And a year later, in February 1973, he noted:

> This committee has a normal staff of sixteen, but actually now there are forty-two members employed by the full committee and its subcommittees. There are indications that even greater numbers may be called for during this Session. A staff of this size is completely

unnecessary and should be reduced, although I doubt that it will be. The chief of the committee's permanent staff, Carl Marcy, appears to have a possessive attitude, does not take too kindly to suggestions for changes in operations of the committee of which he does not first approve.[7]

Despite Senator Aiken's criticism of Marcy, who served as chief of staff of the Foreign Relations Committee from 1955 to 1973, the two men were in agreement—one might even say collusion—about keeping down the size of the committee staff. At a time when many Republicans, tired of their long years in the minority, were demanding separate minority staff representation, Marcy wanted to preserve the nonpartisan nature of the committee staff. Similarly, Senator Aiken always hoped that the committee and its staff could both be operated "as non-partisan in fact as well as in theory" and be held to a modest size. In his oral history, Marcy recalled that his anguish over the creation of a minority staff was mitigated by Senator Aiken. The senator stopped by his office and said, "I know this probably bothers you, but the minority authorized me to pick a staff member who would serve the minority and authorized me to go out and hire such a person if necessary. I want you to know that I have picked Robert Dockery to represent the minority." Marcy was enormously relieved, since Dockery was already a member of the staff and as a result there was no change at all. But as Marcy realized, "It did satisfy a distinct feeling on the part of the minority that they needed to have somebody with whom they could communicate and confide, a feeling that the other members of the staff tended to work mostly for the majority."[8]

Senator Aiken acknowledged that he was not always so successful in arresting the growth of legislative staff. In his valedictory speech to the Senate in December 1974, he confessed his sins as a senator, one of which was to support the expansion of committee staffs "when I knew that an increase was unnecessary and costly." Discussing the Foreign Relations Committee, he asserted,

"I do not believe we need a staff of over 60 members for this committee." He also referred to the "unholy expansion of committees, subcommittees and staff personnel which has mushroomed to an unconscionable extent during the last decade." Although the Legislative Reorganization Act of 1946 had cut the number of committees in half, the number of subcommittees had grown enormously. At the time he left the Senate, there were 144 subcommittees. In response to this proliferation, another reorganization was enacted in 1976 to bring the committees and subcommittees under control—yet the numbers have grown again, placing conflicting committee demands on every senator.9 Milton Young (R–N. Dak.), one of Aiken's Republican colleagues on the Agriculture Committee, complained about having to decide which committee meetings to attend. "I have this problem every day," he said in an oral history. "You try to go to the one that is the most important—the most important to the state. Sometimes you wind up going to two or three in one morning. If you have four or five at the same time, there is just no way you can get to all of them."10

The increasing activities of committees and size of the staff also placed great demands on the Senate's physical plant. When Senator Aiken arrived in Washington, there was a single Senate Office Building. He took room 358, with a view of the building's central courtyard. In the coming years his address changed to the Old Senate Office Building, then the Russell Senate Office Building. He never moved; they just changed the name of the building as new office buildings (known as the SOBs) were added to accommodate growing staff. Although most senators move from office to office to acquire more space and a view of the Capitol dome, Aiken considered his office perfectly adequate and was unwilling to waste taxpayers' money moving to a bigger one with a better view. I should add that in 1965 Senator Aiken acquired a splendid hideaway office in the Capitol with a view of the Washington Monument and downtown Washington. The office became available when Senator Harry Byrd (D–Va.) resigned and several senior Democrats began fighting over who would get this choice space. Finally, someone asked Aiken if he would take it to settle the fight. In his oral history he said he used it "a couple of times a year." But he preferred to work in his own office next to his staff. Later he inherited the office that Margaret Chase Smith had occupied, which he described as "right handy-by to the Senate chamber."[11]

Senator Aiken was initially opposed to the construction of a new Senate Office Building in 1958, believing that the Senate did not need the additional office space. He changed his mind and his vote after he discovered that they planned to use Vermont marble for the structure, now known as the Dirksen Senate Office Building.[12] After he left the Senate, a third office building was added, named for Philip Hart (D–Mich.). Senators still prefer the original Russell Building for its beaux arts grandeur, marble fire-places, mahogany doors, and crystal chandeliers. Neither the Russell nor the Dirksen building was designed for computers and the like, however, and staff members prefer the Hart Building, with its partition walls that can be quickly knocked down, recon-figured, and rewired to fit ever-changing staff needs.

Senator Aiken was at his desk by 7:00 each morning, and by 7:55 he was breakfasting with Senator Mike Mansfield, the Democratic leader, usually over coffee and English muffins in the cafeteria. This twenty-year ritual between a Republican and Democratic senator is part of the folklore of the Senate, everyone wondering what those two exceedingly quiet men talked about every morning.

Aiken and Mansfield began this tradition in the 1950s, when the entire Senate worked out of two buildings: the Capitol and the Senate Office Building, linked together by a subway whose cars resembled wicker baskets. There was a senators' restaurant at the Capitol and a staff cafeteria in the office building. Staff used to gather for coffee and doughnuts in the cafeteria around 10:00 in the morning, and there they got to know their counterparts in other senators' offices and committees. Something of a small-town atmosphere existed. Over the next three decades, the Senate grew from a small town to a large city, with staff spread over several buildings, eating in numerous cafeterias, and lucky to know everyone in their own senator's or committee's office, let alone in other offices. Longtime staff members assert that this loss of community has been detrimental to the legislative process.

Staff members note that in the immediate post–World War II era, senators tended to be more austere—answerable only to God and their constituents—but that they were approachable when a staff member had a good idea. Over the years senators grew less formal; the last cutaway coat disappeared from the Senate with the death of North Carolina senator Clyde Hoey in 1954. Not everyone prefers this informality. The Senate's parliamentarian emeritus, Floyd Riddick, lamented that "the members of the Senate are getting more like the members of the House!" Despite that informality, protective layers of staff now tend to shield senators, making them far less approachable than in the past.13

It used to bother Senator Aiken that new members would show up in the Senate with plans to change the rules and give themselves instant seniority and status in the committees. "It takes quite a while before we realize how much we have to learn about running a democratic government," he commented. Aiken feared that if strict seniority were abandoned, there would be campaigns for the post of chair, which "would be conducted through pressure practices wherein the vested interests, so-called, and ideological organizations would exercise their full power regardless of expense to get persons they feel they could control into strategic positions in the senatorial organization." At another point, when Dee Huddleston, freshman senator from Kentucky, introduced a resolution, Aiken noted he was "a real veteran with six weeks' tenure as a member of the Senate." He regretted that members no longer waited a year or two to make their initial speech and that the tradition of new senators' being seen and not heard did not last long in the age of television (Aiken tended to forget that he delivered his own first speech to the Senate, on lend-lease, only eight weeks after taking his seat).14

George Aiken came to the Senate at a time when it was fairly common for senators to have been governors of their states.

Senator Norris Cotton of New Hampshire recalled how Georgia senator Richard Russell once began a conversation by saying, "When you were governor of your state," until Cotton corrected him that he had never served as governor. Russell was taken aback; a former governor himself, he assumed that most of his colleagues had come up the ladder of state service.[15] Increasingly during Senator Aiken's tenure, senators were less party-selected than self-selected. Televised campaigning brought forward actors, athletes, astronauts, and academics who had never before held public office but gained enough name recognition to win a Senate seat. Far more senators now come out of the House of Representatives than out of statehouses. The staff has also become fertile ground for future senators. Ten of the senators in Congress in 1991 began their Washington careers as staff members in the Senate and House. For that matter, Speaker of the House Tom Foley once worked on the staff of Senator Henry Jackson.

Another facet of the impact of television since the 1950s was the steady increase in numbers of senators seeking to become president of the United States, and the effect that had on absenteeism in the Senate. So far in the twentieth century only Warren G. Harding and John F. Kennedy have gone straight from the Senate to the White House, but think how many others have run: Estes Kefauver, Lyndon Johnson, Hubert Humphrey, Barry Goldwater, Stuart Symington, George McGovern, Henry Jackson, Birch Bayh, Howard Baker, Bob Dole, Tom Harkin, Bob Kerry—the list goes on and on. In January 1972, Senator Aiken confided to his diary:

> I have never seen so many incompetent persons aspiring to high office and apparently well financed in their efforts to achieve it. Some of the subcommittees of important Congressional committees appear to be used largely for the promotion of the aspirations of this or that member of Congress. These subcommittees are granted large appropriations which will be used to a great extent to promote the political aspirations of the

subcommittee chairman. I would be inclined to oppose these appropriations in the Senate were it not for the fact that in the executive branch of government there are many agencies and subagencies which can legally use appropriated funds to insure the reelection of the President.16

A month later he was still complaining of high absenteeism, with thirty or more members gone at a time. He further noted that senators' urge to travel away from Washington seemed stronger in February than at other times of the year. This made it hard to get quorums in committees or on the Senate floor. In March he wrote, "The Friday session of the Senate was not a happy one. There were difficulties in getting a quorum of the Senate at all. Forty-two members were absent. Except for two or three cases of illness the members were out on the road playing politics." But when National Geographic came to photograph the Foreign Relations Committee for the publication *We the People*, Aiken dourly observed that sixteen of the seventeen senators showed up, and the absent member had arranged to have his likeness pasted into the final portrait.17

Congress rose and fell in favor during Senator Aiken's long tenure. For much of his era, the imperial presidency eclipsed Congress in public opinion, until Richard Nixon was humbled by Watergate. Broadcast journalism tended to promote presidents because they were easier to focus on than the collective body of Congress. When Aiken came to Washington, Franklin D. Roosevelt dominated the news from the capital and could address the public directly, over the heads of Congress and the press, via his "fireside chat" radio broadcasts. Strong presidents from Truman to Nixon followed, gaining more space in newspapers and more time on television than was given to the entire legislative branch. Capitol Hill broadcaster Phil Jones of CBS used to lament that he could get senators on television more often if they would just ride around in a fire engine.18

Not that the press ignored Congress. The Senate generally

received more coverage than did the House, and favorable treatment could always be courted by leaking news to selected journalists. Senator Aiken had an office rule against leaks to the press. "I didn't even leak my notice of retirement to the press," he noted proudly. He was sure his office did not leak but could not say the same for the staff members of the committees on which he served. "Staff members do much of the leaking rather than the members of Congress themselves," Senator Aiken commented in his oral history for the University of Vermont. "They get a feeling of importance if they can only leak confidential information to a big newspaper or some news agency." It was a favorite saying of George Aiken's that there were two ways to get status in Washington, especially if one was a member of a committee staff: one was to leak confidential information to a major newspaper or network; the other was to break a leg skiing in Vermont. It seemed to him that whenever someone came back to Washington in a cast, the "victim would be very, very proud."[19]

Like leaks, there were other issues that seemed to be permanent irritants in the legislative process. Raising congressional salaries, for instance, was as difficult during Senator Aiken's career as it is now. He was sympathetic to members who had to rent homes in Washington and raise their families there, but as a man who lived simply and modestly, he disliked moves to raise congressional salaries and opposed proposals to turn the problem over to an independent commission. "I take the position that members of Congress should face the issue themselves rather than transferring responsibility—which is a polite way of saying 'passing the buck,'" he wrote.[20] At the end of his service he voted against a salary increase on the grounds that members were already getting $36,000 a year and any more would only encourage inflation. One can imagine what he would have said had he known that by the early 1990s congressional salaries would be more than triple that amount.

He also disliked the necessity of members' raising money for campaigns all the time. In 1968 Senator Aiken reported spending $17.09 on his reelection campaign, and two years later he told a newspaper reporter: "The Senate is just as strong now as when I came here." Nevertheless, he observed that "a weakness is in the obligation to the campaign contributor, but the public is more aware and more resentful of wrongdoing." Again, the problem has become worse rather than better. Television campaigning has become so necessary and so expensive that senators must raise funds throughout their six-year terms. In 1974, when Aiken chose not to run for reelection, the total expenditures for all Senate candidates was over $28 million; a decade later that figure was closer to $200 million.[21]

In 1974 Aiken turned eighty-two and realized that it was time for him to step aside. The *Burlington Free Press* noted that as Washington changed, Senator Aiken became "symbolic of a Vermont-styled eccentricity. He was the longest sitting member of the most exclusive club in the country, but he maintained a fresh perspective on ordinary people. His aides were small town folks running a small office in the capital of the most powerful nation on earth. After a while, they felt increasingly out of place."[22]

At the end of his tenure, he was pleased when some seventy senators took the floor to speak about his service, but he noted: "Going back to Vermont will not be as difficult as they seem to think it ought to be." He seemed surprised to find that his pension check amounted to more than his Senate paycheck. Had he resigned a few days early, before December 31, 1974, his annuity would have been 7.4 percent higher. But he chose not to do so. He believed in carrying out contracts in full. When he started his career, he had sacrificed some Senate seniority by waiting a week before beginning his term, so that he could complete his term as governor of Vermont and deliver his farewell address—and advice—to the incoming legislature. He had never regretted his action, and he was determined to conclude his Senate service with the same sense of duty.[23]

The Senate as an institution changed dramatically during George Aiken's years and not always in directions that he approved. As it changed, he remained steadfastly the same, a rugged individual to the end. In Senate parlance, he was a workhorse rather than a show horse. He spent his time on the Agriculture Committee, doing the legislative business that he enjoyed the most, and on the Foreign Relations Committee, doing the business that he probably enjoyed the least. He served in the minority for thirty of his thirty-four years, but when he spoke, especially in closed committee meetings, his words carried great weight on both sides of the aisle. It seems only appropriate to use George Aiken as a measure of the transformation that took place during his third of a century in the U.S. Senate, since in the words of his regular breakfast companion, Mike Mansfield, "George was an institution unto himself."[24]

Senator Aiken and staff, June 1971. Left to right: Stephen Terry, Therese Lepine, Elizabeth Quinn, Senator Aiken, Charlie Weaver, Maryann McKinney, Lola Aiken, Ellen Jones, Pat Terpstra, Marion Whitney. Not shown: Joanna Bell. Courtesy of Bailey/Howe Library, University of Vermont.

4

George Aiken: A Senate Diary

Stephen C. Terry

I WANT TO OFFER A PERSONAL RETROSPECTIVE ON THE
life of George D. Aiken, focusing in particular on what it
was like to work for him by describing a typical day for
Aiken and his staff. I refer primarily to his last term in office, from
April 1969 to January 1975, when I was his legislative assistant.

It has been almost two decades since I left room 358 in the
old Senate Office Building, now known as the Russell Senate
Office Building, to return to Vermont. In the intervening period
I have thought a lot about George Aiken, and in 1989 one of my
colleagues, Bill Porter, and I began to organize our recollections
and research in order to write a biography of him. I started with
firsthand observations of Senator Aiken's last term and have been
steadily researching my way backward through his long public
career. The journey has been fascinating. I am discovering qualities about Aiken that I never knew. I am discovering aspects of his
life that I never suspected, even though I spent six years working
close by his side. As any biographer will tell you, recreating a life

is not an easy task. Hardly a day goes by in my own life that I don't reflect on current events and try to imagine how Aiken would have voted on them or what he would have said about them.

Senator Aiken had no intention of serving a sixth term in the U.S. Senate. In 1968, when he was in his fifth term, he was seventy-six years old. He had already been in public life in one capacity or another since 1931. He wanted to retire, and if there was any political leader who had earned the right to go back to his home on West Hill in Putney to tend to his gardens, write, and think, it was George Aiken. His good friend Senator Mike Mansfield prevailed upon him to seek a sixth and final term. But Lola and Aiken also made themselves a promise that if elected, which seemed very likely, he would not run again at age eighty-two. Aiken kept that decision a closely guarded secret until February 1974, the middle of his sixth term, when he finally announced to the world what he had been thinking about for more than six years—that it was time "to go home to complete some unfinished business."

Aiken was first elected to the Senate in 1940 and served until January 1975. By the end of his career, he was widely acknowledged to be the dean of the Senate and one of the most influential members of that body. He was not powerful in the sense of Lyndon Johnson or Richard Russell, senator from Georgia. His influence was based on his personal integrity, his wit, and his friendship with Mansfield.

He worked quietly, person to person; he built alliances; and he was always concerned about making sure the other party could save face. This ability to bring people together to find a common ground became a hallmark of his career. That is why in 1963 President John F. Kennedy insisted that Aiken be part of the U.S. delegation that went to Moscow to sign the first nuclear test ban treaty. Kennedy knew that in order to get the treaty confirmed by the U.S. Senate, he needed bipartisan support. Aiken helped him achieve that.

It was in this same spirit that in 1964 President Johnson turned to Aiken to help bring together a small group of senators to develop the compromise that allowed the passage and enactment of the president's landmark civil rights bill. Aiken's contribution to the law was in the public accommodations section, in which he carved out an exemption for "Mrs. Murphy's boarding house." This exemption stated that any person who rents four or fewer rooms did not fall under the jurisdiction of the public accommodation law. That compromise broke the logjam and cleared the way for enacting historic legislation that extended the role of federal government to protect the civil rights of all Americans.

A Typical Day in the U.S. Senate

Senator Aiken was an early riser. He said it was the result of getting up to milk cows and do chores on the family farm during his childhood. As a farm boy, George Aiken was also used to working long hours. His Senate schedule reflected that. On a typical Saturday, Senator Aiken along with members of his staff would arrive at 6:45 A.M. From 1972 to 1975, Aiken used every Saturday morning to write and dictate his Senate diary, which he later published as a book. His diary was a running commentary on the turbulent years of change in the Senate that came about as a result of controversies over Vietnam and Nixon's resignation. Monday through Friday Senator Aiken followed a similarly regular schedule in Washington.

5:00–6:45 A.M.: Up in the Morning Early

The Aikens lived in the Methodist Building located on the corner of Constitution Avenue and C Street. Aiken's office was located just across the street. After a bowl of cereal, while Lola was getting ready, Aiken worked on one of the jigsaw puzzles he was always in the process of assembling. Sometimes he used this time to make notes on a white legal pad that he kept on a bed stand. (On many occasions the senator would wake up in the middle of the night to write down an idea for a speech or a piece of legislation.)

On his way to the office, Aiken would stop at the U.S. Capitol lawn to feed peanuts to the squirrels and pigeons, a routine he very much enjoyed.

6:45–7:50 A.M.: *The First Work of the Day*

More often than not, Aiken would be the first to arrive in the office. Executive secretary Elizabeth Quinn or I would usually be there before 7:00 A.M. Senator Aiken began the day by scanning the Vermont newspapers or perhaps calling a family member in Vermont. By 7:30, Lola and Betty Quinn would have opened the first mail; after the senator read it, letters were placed in a box on Lola's desk for Quinn, executive assistant Charles Weaver, or me to answer. Quinn took mail relating to social and speaking engagements, requests for tourist visits, and information about the Capitol. Weaver handled correspondence about agriculture and nuclear energy. I responded to letters relating to foreign policy, environmental matters, and defense issues and requests by Vermont state agencies for help in dealings with the federal government. After Weaver retired in 1972, I also dealt with most of the agricultural legislation, and Betsy Samuelson attended to the other topic areas he had formerly covered.

7:50–8:30 A.M: *Breakfast—More Than a Meal*

Aiken, Lola, Quinn, Samuelson, and I went by the subway to the U.S. Capitol for coffee at the Senate Dining Room. Aiken and Lola ate breakfast at a special table reserved for them and Senator Mansfield. There, over coffee and English muffins, the three of them discussed the events of the day or talked about the Washington social scene. The Aiken-Mansfield breakfast became a Washington institution; it occurred almost every working day for more than twenty years. It was Aiken's special relationship with Mansfield, the majority leader, that gave the Vermonter access to all of the decisions regarding Senate floor action. Aiken and Mansfield never told one another how they would vote but did discuss how they thought the Senate would react to certain votes and issues. Outsiders were rarely allowed to join the tête-à-tête.

8:30–10:00 A.M.: Office Work

After breakfast Aiken and the staff returned to our desks to prepare for the day's events. Senator Aiken usually had an hour and a half before his first committee meeting. At this time he met with constituents who had scheduled appointments, Vermont state officials who were in town, or executive branch officials. More often than not, however, he and the staff went over the legislative calendar, upcoming votes, and action for the coming day. By then, I had ready a half-page memo on the breaking news events in Vermont, information I usually obtained by early-morning calls to Bill Porter, managing editor of the *Times Argus,* or Norm James, news director at WDEV in Waterbury. Because Aiken had the top news of the day, he was able to converse in a very up-to-the-minute way with any Vermonter, constituent or state official, who called from home.

10:00 A.M.–Noon: Committee Work

Aiken began his round of committee meetings by midmorning. His habit was to stop at the Agriculture Committee, located on the third floor of the Russell Senate Office Building, to see the agenda for the day. If the committee hearings involved dairy legislation, rural development, the farm bill, or forest service issues, he stayed and participated. From there, he walked to the U.S. Capitol Building and the Senate Foreign Relations Committee, where, as ranking Republican member, he attended committee hearings. From 1969 to January 1975, the Foreign Relations Committee dominated Aiken's agenda, primarily because it dealt with many vexing foreign policy issues. These included extensive hearings on the Vietnam War and constitutional issues such as the War Powers Act, the National Commitments Treaty, the antiballistic missile system, and repeal of the Tonkin Gulf Resolution.

Noon–5:30 P.M.: In the Senate

The Senate began its session in the afternoon. Aiken usually went to the Senate floor to check on the orders of the day, then repaired to the private Senate Dining Room, located across from the public Senate Dining Room in the Capitol. Lunch usually consisted of a cup of soup, a sandwich, and a dish of chocolate ice cream. Depending on the schedule of the Senate, Aiken would either spend the afternoon on the floor or return to his committee meetings. In between these meetings, he sandwiched more appointments with Vermont constituents or executive branch officials.

On a typical day a family from Vermont would stop by the senator's office. If Aiken was there, he would always step out into the anteroom to greet the family, make arrangements to get them a White House pass, or have a staff member escort them to the visitors' gallery of the U.S. Senate. If, as on so many occasions, Aiken was walking over to the U.S. Senate, he would accompany the visitors to the gallery. On some occasions, when the line was long or there was a delay getting in, Aiken took his constituents to the special Senate family gallery and asked that they be let in.

While Aiken was attending committee meetings or on the Senate floor, his staff remained in the office processing the mail, sitting in on committee hearings for him, and working on Vermont problems. Senator Aiken had no designated press secretary, but Lola or I filled that function. Lola was the administrative assistant, a position she held from 1944 to January 1975, when she, too, retired and left Washington. When George Aiken married Lola Pierotti in July 1967, she was making $27,000 a year. She went off the Senate payroll, but she certainly did not stop working, serving nine years as an unpaid administrative assistant—a rare case in a Congress where many senators have relatives on the congressional payroll.

Senator Aiken wrote almost all his own speeches. Although a staff member prepared a draft, the senator would simply take the ideas and dictate a whole new speech from top to bottom. George Aiken was a graceful writer. He never wrote complicated sentences; he wrote simple and direct prose. On many occasions he did not prepare formal speeches, reserving them for major addresses in the U.S. Senate. He used to say the only reason that he wrote a speech was to make sure that he "wouldn't forget to say what [he] wanted to." But for the most part, he often remarked, he rarely knew what he was going to say before he stood up to talk.

There were two things he minded most about giving a speech: "the first was getting started, and the other was stopping. The in-between was rarely a problem." His preferred strategy was to use three-by-five-inch index cards that set out facts or suggested starting points on a variety of topics. When he returned to Vermont for an extended period that included speaking engagements, he brought along his index cards. On a blank card he would write down three or four points he wanted to make to a particular audience he was scheduled to address. His speeches always included some local story or mention of an incident that happened to him in that spot as much as ten, twenty, or thirty years earlier. He often took questions from the audience.

Another favorite technique was to bring the morning newspaper to the event. Aiken would stand up before the crowd and provide a running commentary on the news behind the headlines. He interspersed these observations with insights about the people and personalities in Washington and with a special wry sense of humor that came from looking at an event from the long view of history.

5:30–11:00 P.M.: The Social Scene

The Senate officially closed at 5:30 P.M., but in the early 1970s the senators frequently worked into the evening. Lola went home, and I stayed with the senator. At 6:00 he and I went to his hideaway office off the Senate floor for a cocktail. Then we would have dinner in the Senate Dining Room, where Aiken ate sparingly: a hamburger, french fries or cole slaw, a dish of chocolate ice cream, and milk. I remained with the senator on the Senate floor, sitting in the handsome leather couches at the back of the chamber reserved for staff with floor privileges. When the day's work ended, I walked home with him.

If the Aikens were invited to an embassy or private dinner party—and if the Senate was not in session—Aiken left the office at 5:30 to change into his tuxedo; he stayed at the function until about 11:00 P.M. He did this two or three nights a week, more so after he became dean of the Senate. Aiken was a favorite guest of Washington hostesses. His distinctive red tie and Yankee humor were well known in the capital and on the social pages of the *Washington Post* and the *Evening Star.* His expert knowledge of wildflowers, fruits, and berries always found its way into cocktail and dinner conversation.

George Aiken was also a favorite of the Washington media. He was a source of information and sometimes the source of unattributed Washington gossip, especially for the writers of the Washington "Whispers" column that appears in *U.S. News and World Report.* He almost always spoke for the record. He was the master of the one-liner even before sound bites came into vogue. After Nixon ordered the invasion of Cambodia in May 1970, for example, Aiken opined that the Republican party that fall "could not get elected dog catcher."

One central theme that ran throughout Aiken's career was his abiding concern for his home state of Vermont. Almost every piece of legislation, almost every action, and almost every speech he gave (unless it was strictly foreign policy) would likely contain a reference to or be put in the context of how it would affect the folks in Vermont.

Aiken had an unerring instinct for the political views of his constituents. The Vermont that George Aiken knew in the 1920s and 1930s was rapidly changing to the Vermont of the 1960s, 1970s, and 1980s. But Aiken was never afraid of change because his roots went deep in the Green Mountains. He could swing to the left, to the right, or stand up squarely in the middle; he could compromise; he could take the long view. But there remained a bedrock of truths that served as a solid foundation for his public life.

Above all, Aiken believed that people are people the world

over and that the job of government is to give all people a voice. He believed that the citizen at the low end of the economic scale has just as much right to power as the citizen at the top end of the scale. Aiken was committed to making education available to all segments of society. He was also committed to protecting natural resources, which he believed were a common heritage and were not to be used for the special interests of the few. That philosophy was inherent in his fight in the 1930s against flood control legislation plans of the Roosevelt administration, his passionate desire to open up the Northeast Kingdom for recreational use, and his proposal in his last year in office to create eastern wilderness areas so citizens of the East, like the citizens west of the Mississippi, could enjoy the forest primeval.

Although he was a lifelong and loyal Republican, George Aiken was also a democrat. He passionately believed that people could change their government. But to do that politicians had to start at the most logical place. Political careers, in his view, had to begin in local organizations. If you could prove yourself to your own people—if your friends and neighbors voted for you—then you had a political future. His long career in politics and his daily routine in the U.S. Senate were both a continual test and confirmation of those beliefs.

A birthday card to Aiken from a Senate page, "your young Friend, Werth,"
June 20, 1946. Courtesy of Bailey/Howe Library, University of Vermont.

5

George Aiken, Senator from Vermont

Anna Kasten Nelson

T HE READER WHO SCANS THE SHELVES OF A BOOK-
store or library will find no shortage of books on the
presidency, individual presidents, or presidential administrations. Biographies of senators or books devoted to their senatorial careers, however, sit in lonely isolation on half-empty
shelves. At first glance it seems a curious anomaly. Each day that
Congress is in session, a senator prepares remarks and questions
witnesses in hearings that become part of the public record.
Speeches on the Senate floor, even though doctored before they
reach the *Congressional Record,* also are readily available. Recorded
votes help to reveal public policy positions, and speeches back
home indicate the concerns of the electorate. As a result, the views
of members of Congress are a part of the public record; in contrast, presidents' decisions and opinions are "released" only after
being sifted through layers of staff.

Nevertheless, we continue to ask questions and seek answers about legislators and the legislative process that cannot be answered by the public record; we continue to find it difficult to understand senatorial careers. Given the lively interest in public figures, why do members of the Senate remain so elusive? In many ways George Aiken's career is illustrative of the problem.

Aiken's was a very long career. When he was first elected to Congress in 1940, there were roughly 133.4 million people in the country, 23 percent of whom were designated by the census as part of the farm population.[1] In spite of the proliferation of "alphabet agencies" during the New Deal period, the capital that was to become his home for so much of the time in the years ahead was still a sleepy, small southern town. Its lack of sophistication was personified by its only airport, Hoover Field, which was finally replaced in time for World War II; one observer described it as "little more than a grassy field between an amusement park on one side and a warehouse and dump area on the other."[2] A highway ran across the solitary runway, and despite many attempts to change the situation, for years "pilots flew in and out of Washington timing their landings to coincide with breaks" in the highway traffic.

The Senate Aiken entered in what would prove to be the momentous year of 1941 was poorly equipped to challenge the growing domination of the executive branch. Although the installation of air-conditioning allowed for longer sessions, in other ways the pace of Congress continued to be leisurely. The legislators whom Aiken joined were as unprepared for the coming war and its aftermath as was the rest of the country. In addition, Aiken joined a Republican minority at a time when longevity of tenure was the hallmark of southern senators from one-party Democratic states, who thus controlled many of the committees and much of the leadership.

By the time Aiken retired, thirty-four years later, the United States had fought three major wars; the national security costs of fighting the cold war had escalated to consume unprecedented chunks of the nation's budget; and the United States had been governed by six presidents, having seen one of those presidents assassinated, one forced from office, and one threatened with impeachment. Each of these presidents, in implementing his agenda, had added to the agencies, civil servants, and political appointees in the executive branch. Meanwhile, as the machinery of government became more and more unwieldy, the White House staff increased in numbers and power.

In response to the domination of the executive branch, congressional staffs grew exponentially and became far more partisan. Although Senator Aiken continued to win elections with low campaign budgets and little hype, senatorial candidates competing in populous states served by numerous television stations often sacrificed public policy to the needs of their financial backers. Other senators, capitalizing on national name recognition, sacrificed public policy to promote their political futures.

Meanwhile, a highly urban population experienced a revolution in civil rights, social mores, and dramatic changes in the workplace and the nature of work. Even more to the point when we consider Aiken's background and constituency, fewer than 4 percent of the American people could still be classified as farmers by 1975.[3]

Like many first-termers, Aiken was given initial committee assignments that were hardly prestigious. He became a member of the Committee on Expenditures in the Executive Departments (later the Committee on Government Operations) and even chaired that committee from 1947 to 1948, when the Republicans briefly controlled Congress. He also served on the Committee on Labor and Public Welfare and chaired the Subcommittee on Education. He shared President Truman's interest in an efficient government, and he was genuinely concerned about issues facing each of his other committees. The major issues for the administration and the Congress after 1941, however, revolved around winning World War II and waging the cold war, which meant allocating federal funds to further either the country's domestic programs or its global interests, choosing between domestic agencies and military services responsible for national security.

It was not until 1954, more than a dozen years after he entered Congress, that Aiken became involved in these central issues by moving onto the Foreign Relations Committee and, in 1959, onto the Joint Committee on Atomic Energy. For the remainder of his career, his seniority as well as his judgment and integrity gave him entrée, if he so desired, to the power centers of Washington.

There was, of course, one committee above all others that occupied Aiken throughout his senatorial career. He joined the Committee on Agriculture in 1941, serving as chairman from 1953 to 1954 (when the Republicans again briefly captured Congress) and leaving the committee as ranking minority member only when he retired.

Aiken's commitment to the Agriculture Committee illustrates an important point about his lengthy career in the Senate. As he faced the challenges of the wars, scandals, social upheavals, assassinations, and other changes that whirled about him, Senator George Aiken in his personal and political response never really left Vermont. This is not to label Aiken as either provincial or parochial but to contribute to an understanding of his views and actions as senator. It explains the basic consistency that marked his career. Indeed, those who comment that Aiken was a hard man to label miss the point. He was invariably true to his own experiences and those of his neighbors. It is especially interesting to see how Aiken took that background and moved it into the realm of national public policy.

In his oral history memoir, Aiken declared that he ran for the Vermont House of Representatives, his first statewide office, to stop the utility companies from "buying every dam site on almost every brook in Vermont where they could generate five hundred kilowatts of power."4 He had already experienced what he regarded as the deceitfulness of the New England Power Company. It had promised to serve East Putney and then announced that the local folks would have to pay for the transmitter—a cost that was beyond the means of the population.5 Throughout his career Aiken remained suspicious of utility companies and all other corporations that owned the fossil fuels in the country or monopolized hydroelectric power. And he sought to achieve adequate energy sources at low rates for the New England region.

He never forgot that the private power companies consistently refused to serve rural areas as they brought electricity to the nation in the 1930s. Even before he reached the Senate, Aiken was a proponent of the Rural Electrification Administration and supported the low-interest loans that sustained the rural electric cooperatives. Toward the end of his career, Aiken continued to introduce bills for low-interest loans to the cooperatives. Finally, when it became clear that government financing at 2 percent interest was no longer feasible, he sponsored legislation to provide the electric and telephone cooperatives with a special fund from which they could continue to borrow without federal loans.[6]

As a member of the Government Operations Committee, Aiken had another opportunity to defend low-cost energy when he served on the Commission on Organization of the Executive Branch, generally known as the Hoover Commission. President Truman established the commission to rationalize the proliferation of agencies his administration inherited from the New Deal and World War II. Aiken was by no means the dominant figure on the commission, and his tenure is easily overlooked, even though he was always keen on limiting the power of the executive branch. But he did not hesitate to file dissenting opinions when he disagreed with the reports of the commission task forces that proposed government withdrawal from the production of electric power. In one instance he supported the continuation of government lending agencies such as the Rural Electrification Administration in the face of recommendations that they be curtailed. In another he wrote that two of the reports "follow so closely the arguments which the private power interests present in opposition to public water-resource development that the general welfare viewpoint does not seem to be properly represented.... The power companies exploit our water resources almost solely for the production of electric energy, with profit as the basic consideration."[7]

Aiken understood that energy, and in particular low-cost

electricity, were just as essential to the well-being of rural Americans as to city dwellers. That awareness led him into other battles that proved as important to the country as they were to his neighbors. One of those was the St. Lawrence Seaway and Power Project. Support for the project was so high on his agenda that he first introduced a bill to construct the project in 1943—in the midst of World War II. It took eleven years and many more attempts before the necessary legislation was finally passed. Aiken, of course, was primarily interested in the hydroelectric power the project would generate for New England. As he emphasized his support for the project, he characteristically noted that the major opposition came from the "power interests" as well as the railroads.[8] The pleasure he took in reporting the low cost of electricity the St. Lawrence project ultimately provided for Vermont is clear from his oral history interview. Yet few would deny that the development of the St. Lawrence Seaway was a significant economic investment with ramifications far beyond the borders of New England.[9] Once again Aiken had worked from his own experience to promote public policy that benefited the entire nation.[10]

In 1959 Aiken was appointed to the Joint Committee on Atomic Energy and joined those who enthusiastically supported nuclear power as an alternate form of energy. He never quite believed critics who warned of the dangers of nuclear power plants, as those opponents included his old enemies: the coal and oil producers.

Underlying Aiken's entire career in Washington was his concern with agricultural policy, land use, and the American farmer. Although a Vermont senator traditionally serves on the Committee on Agriculture, Aiken had a personal bond with the land, and his concern with the economy of Vermont dominated his views. To achieve his goals in a Senate led by Democrats, he worked in tandem with members as disparate as Committee Chairman Allen Ellender of Louisiana and Hubert Humphrey of Minnesota, whose constituents shared many of the same economic problems with Vermonters.[11]

Aiken cosponsored, promoted, or opposed an enormous volume of agricultural acts, each one more arcane than the one before. Throughout his tenure Aiken was against the policy of scarcity advocated by many farm leaders eager to protect the economic livelihood of the farmer. As early as 1947, Aiken argued that a hungry world (and, it would later appear, a hungry nation) needed U.S. farm surpluses. The challenge as he saw it was not to find ways to promote scarcity but to expand world markets to absorb the abundance produced in this country.[12] Aiken often stated that he joined the Foreign Relations Committee because "no two committees ... tie more closely together than Foreign Relations and Agriculture. You cannot consider an agricultural program of the United States without considering foreign relations and what is going on in the rest of the world."[13] Therefore Aiken was a cosponsor of Public Law 480. Under this act, the U.S. government could buy surplus commodities and then sell them for local currencies to countries that had no U.S. dollars—often the hungriest countries in Africa and Asia, the so-called Third World nations of the cold war era.

In support of PL 480, Aiken argued that it would increase world trade, add to economic prosperity around the world, and hence serve as a strong deterrent to war.[14] Even though it did none of these, PL 480 did help both feed the growing world population and relieve the plight of the American farmer by keeping the huge agricultural surpluses from depressing the market price for these commodities.[15]

Membership on the Foreign Relations Committee brought Aiken into a world even farther from Putney than had his life in Washington up to that time. He served as a member of the U.S. delegation to the United Nations General Assembly and traveled to Latin America and Southeast Asia. Presidents of both parties invited him to briefings at the White House. He responded to dinner invitations from the diplomatic community and had visits from foreign dignitaries who wished to influence U.S. policy toward their countries.[16]

Few would disagree with the conclusion that George Aiken's contributions to public policy were most impressive in what might be regarded as the middle years of his long tenure. In a legislative body that rewarded seniority, he could exert little leadership until after World War II. But in the next two decades he effectively protected the interests of rural America, fostered the completion of the St. Lawrence Seaway, and saw the introduction of PL 480. In the final decade of his Senate career, he moved more and more into foreign policy as the wrenching experience of the Vietnam War began to reach every corner of America. Although honored for his integrity and respected for his views, Aiken had few experiences to draw upon in his new role as an elder statesman on the Foreign Relations Committee. Hence his position was more often that of a supporter of policies rather than a leader.

Aiken donated his papers to a public university, left us a "diary" of his last three years in the Senate, and graciously agreed to be interviewed for an oral history memoir. Why, then, does our view of George Aiken's public career, like that of many other senators, remain so hazy? What are we seeking? What else do we want to know?

First, we wish to know more about the political process itself. Did Aiken assemble the coalitions that passed his proposals? How did he use those brief years as a member of the majority party? In the final analysis was it the support of President Eisenhower that assured the passage of the St. Lawrence Seaway?

Second, although we come to know George Aiken of Putney, Vermont, as we read his oral interview transcript and diary, these passages do not always help us understand George Aiken, U.S. senator. For example, he told about Richard Nixon and the Watergate affair but not what he thought or felt about them. Yet because he was a lifelong Republican and loyal Nixon supporter, the scandal must have been a trying experience. He writes warmly of Agriculture Committee chairman Ellender, but what could he have thought of Ellender's segregationist views? Nor do we ever discover whether or how Aiken's travels and United Nations experience influenced his votes or changed his views.

The gaps in our understanding may never be adequately filled, even if the biographers scour every possible source. Aiken, however, would probably view the entire issue as irrelevant. His words are readily available in congressional documents, and his accomplishments show clearly in the legislation he sponsored and cosponsored as well as the votes he cast on the Senate floor. No doubt he would characterize those of us who ask for more as he did the bluejays he enjoyed watching in Putney. "Birds are so much like people," he wrote. "The blue jay, for instance, after stealing and storing everything he can possibly need, continues to keep grabbing for more."[17]

*Aiken in his Senate office, June 28, 1967. Photo by WCAX-TV. Courtesy of
Bailey/Howe Library, University of Vermont.*

6

The World in Aiken's Times: The Rise and Decline of the United States

Thomas G. Paterson

*T*HE WORLD KNEW LITTLE PEACE DURING GEORGE Aiken's years in the U.S. Senate. World War II raged throughout Europe and Asia, ensnaring the rest of the globe in its fury when Aiken journeyed to Washington in 1941 to assume his new position. When Senator Aiken returned to Vermont in 1975 after thirty-four years in the upper house of Congress, Middle East tensions stretched taut; the world economy wobbled, rocked by high oil prices; famine wracked Africa; Southeast Asia lay bloodied from years of civil war and outside intervention; and the costly cold war, despite steps toward détente, ground on. In those three decades, an unrelenting series of crises fed fears and scares—not only of nuclear annihilation but of economic cataclysm, starvation, and social upheaval.

As ideologies and empires clashed, national security managers everywhere grappled with disorder, seeking mechanisms to calm and pacify or launching military campaigns to coerce and dominate. Client-state wars, revolutions, terrorism, insurgencies, economic embargoes, and religious and ethnic conflicts prompted leaders to fear chain reactions that might ultimately—in the language of the domino theory—topple the last big dominoes themselves, the Soviet Union and the United States. Presidents during Aiken's tenure, from Franklin D. Roosevelt to Gerald R. Ford, struggled to define America's place in this chaotic international system and to defend and expand U.S. interests abroad in a world at constant war.

The Senate career of George Aiken, then, intersected with momentous global events and trends that set his and the nation's foreign policy agenda. In this essay I describe the environment in which the Vermont senator had to make decisions, examining the four significant eras that he witnessed and to some degree shaped: first, the growth and expansion of American power and the globalization of U.S. foreign policy in the 1940s—the era of World War II and the early cold war; second, the rise of the Third World in the 1950s as decolonization and revolutionary nationalism created a host of new, independent, and often neutralist states that challenged the two superpowers and diffused world power; third, the tragedy of Vietnam, that wrenching war in the 1960s that staggered all combatants and etched itself upon American memory; and, fourth, the challenge to U.S. hegemony in the 1970s—a consequence in large part of the first three changes. An understanding of these moments in international history will help us explain the overarching theme in Aiken's time: the rise and relative decline of the United States as the predominant power in the world.

American entry into World War II, a truly global war, transformed the United States into a global power with a global foreign policy. For the first time in its history, the United States took on major international responsibilities, sent a massive military juggernaut to distant continents, and seized opportunities to command the direction of world affairs. With pledges of "no more

Munichs" and "no more Pearl Harbors," U.S. leaders vowed to prevent a replay of the 1930s—that time when economic depression spawned political extremism and war. They promised an unprecedented diplomatic activism and a global watchdog role for a United States that had once spurned international leadership of first rank. Emerging from its isolationism, America had a second chance. Now, as one historian has described Secretary of State Dean Acheson's understanding of the opportunity, "only the United States had the power to grab hold of history and make it conform."[1]

World War II was so ravaging, total, and profound that it overturned a world system. Besides causing 55 million deaths, the war left much of Europe and Asia in rubble. Displaced people wandered in search of food and family. Transportation and communications lay in ruins. Devastated factories and farms demonstrated the ferocity of bombing raids and marching armies. Politics descended into disarray as competing factions—in Poland, Greece, and China—vied for power to remake their societies.

The upending of the old order became evident, too, in the disintegration of empires: Britain's India, France's Indochina, the Netherlands' Indonesia, and more. With Britain bankrupt and Germany, Italy, and Japan defeated, the world map was redrawn and power in the international system was redistributed. The United States and the Soviet Union, with quite different ideologies, emerged to claim high rank. Their competition polarized world politics in what soon became known as the cold war.

President Harry S Truman's decision to drop atomic bombs on Japan, moreover, unleashed a nuclear arms race that became a central feature of the postwar era, a haunting specter of doomsday. With the advent of the air age, the globe shrank. A long-range bomber could easily cover the distance to another country and deliver its payload by surprise. "We are for all time de-isolated," said one observer.[2] The United States, unlike much of the rest of the world, survived World War II not only intact but strengthened. No bombs fell on its northeastern industrial plants; no tanks rumbled through midwestern grainfields. The U.S. economy expanded tremendously during the war, the gross national product jumping from $90 billion to $212 billion. By 1948, Americans produced 41 percent of the world's goods and services.[3] The United States so outdistanced other nations in almost every measurement of power, from industrial production to military forces to political stability, that historians say it enjoyed hegemony in the postwar world—hegemony existing when one nation has such a strong economy that it can maintain a strong military, which in turn helps it to exert compelling political influence. More than statistics established U.S. supremacy; world conditions did so: the United States was powerful because almost everybody else was weak.

The cold war—a contest between the Soviet Union and the United States to establish spheres of influence—fixed itself upon the international system in those years. From Poland to Greece, China to Korea, Truman Doctrine to Marshall Plan, NATO to Warsaw Pact—issues upon which Senator Aiken cast votes—the Soviet-U.S. confrontation dominated world politics. Cold war America became obsessed with communism, exaggerating its influence at home and abroad. The United States girded the globe with economic and military alliances to thwart perceived adversaries. Americans also vigorously advanced their ideology of open-door capitalism and political democracy and used the United Nations Organization as an instrument for U.S. goals. Americans came to dominate the world economy through World Bank loans, foreign aid, exports, and overseas investments.

Truman was pleased to observe in 1947 that the United States was "the giant of the economic world," but a British magazine, the *Economist*, worried that "the United States now towers above its fellows. Like mice in the cage of an elephant, they follow with apprehension the movements of the mammoth. What chance would they stand if it were to begin to throw its weight around, they who are in danger even if it only decides to sit down?"[4] Senator J. William Fulbright (D–Ark.) would later disparage an American "arrogance of power."[5] Wars and repeated foreign interventions—both direct and covert—became familiar U.S.

practice: Iran in 1946, Greece and Turkey in 1947, Italy in 1948, Korea in 1950, Iran again in 1953, Guatemala in 1954, and more.

On the domestic front Americans debated the uses and methods of their international power. Those leaders who insisted that the containment doctrine be implemented primarily by military means won the day, as a chagrined George Aiken learned well. The Vermont senator also participated in the development of bipartisanship in matters of foreign policy. Bipartisanship blunted criticisms of U.S. policies in the interests of presenting a united front to the Soviets. Aiken somberly observed, moreover, the growing authority of the president in the system of checks and balances—in short, the growth of the imperial presidency. Congress yielded more and more power to the executive branch—including the constitutional authority to declare war—and found itself unable to monitor many agencies in the government, including the Central Intelligence Agency, founded in 1947. The acronym for the CIA, complained some, meant "Congress Isn't Aware."6 As Senator Aiken remarked on the question of congressional oversight of covert actions, "That was a joke."7 Excessive secrecy in the name of national security, another cost of the cold war, made it difficult for Americans, including members of the U.S. Senate, to hold their government accountable. Aiken, Mike Mansfield, and other senators chafed under the restraints imposed by cold war fears.

If Senator Aiken experienced the United States' rise to global power in the cold war 1940s, he also watched the rise of the Third World in the next decade. The Third World challenged the bipolar configuration of world power, and he and others on the Senate Foreign Relations Committee had to search for policies to meet this new phenomenon. After the war a cavalcade of colonies broke from their imperial rulers. From 1943 to 1989 no fewer than ninety-six countries gained independence and entered the international system as new states. Many liberations came in the 1950s: Libya in 1951; Sudan, Morocco, and Tunisia in 1956; Ghana in 1957. In 1960 alone eighteen new African nations became independent.

Analysts at first called them backward or underdeveloped nations, then shifted to less-disparaging terms like *developing* or *emerging* states. Soon countries became members of the "Third World," those parts of the global community belonging neither to the "First World" of the United States and its allies in the capitalist "West" nor to the "Second World" of the Soviet Union and its allies in the Communist "East." Third World nations, including many states long independent in Latin America, were largely nonwhite, nonindustrialized, poor, and located in the southern half of the globe. A number became unstable nations plagued by civil wars; dictatorial rulers; tribal, ethnic, and class rivalries; famine; and dependency on the sale of only one commodity.

Many Third World states joined the nonaligned movement initiated at the Bandung conference of 1955. Third World expressions of separation from the two major powers came in many other forms, including Pan-Arabism and Muslim fundamentalism, the Group of Seventy-seven in the United Nations, and the call for a law of the sea treaty to ensure that rich seabed minerals did not become profit for commercial mining companies alone.

Third World states became a formidable bloc in global forums, and the United States gradually became isolated in the United Nations. In the Security Council, for example, losing the majority vote its allies and clients had long provided, the United States had to cast its first veto in 1970. By the 1980s, in the General Assembly, the United States cast the largest number of negative votes. Third World nations also threw the U.S.-designed liberal, capitalist order on the defensive in the 1970s by demanding a new international economic order in which the industrialized nations of the "North" would share their wealth with the "South" through tariff revision, technology transfers, and increased economic assistance.

As the Third World became an important force, the international system fragmented, bipolarism eroded, and the relative power of both the United States and the Soviet Union diminished accordingly. The superpowers inevitably but gradually yielded some ground to the Third World. International affairs became more fluid, more unpredictable, less secure, and less manageable. U.S. policymakers launched economic and military programs to woo these new nations to the U.S. camp. By 1961, 90 percent of U.S. foreign aid went to the Third World. So much seemed at stake: sites for military bases and intelligenceposts, markets, sources of strategic raw materials, and votes in international agencies. Yet the United States faced a number of handicaps in this battle for the hearts and minds of Third World peoples. The first obstacle was U.S. unwillingness to accept Third World states on their own terms, as neutrals in the cold war. They did not wish to become subservient clients or battlegrounds for superpower contests. "We haven't gotten rid of one imperialism to take on another one," declared Egypt's Gamal Abdul Nasser, one of the leaders of the nonaligned movement.[8] Secretary of State John Foster Dulles pronounced neutralism immoral, charging that it was a first step along the road to communism. Take sides or else, he warned.

The United States' domestic race relations also obstructed Washington's efforts to win favor in the Third World. Segregation and discriminatory practices common in the United States repeatedly insulted foreign diplomats of color. In the 1950s, to cite a few examples, the ambassador from India was told to leave a whites-only restaurant at the Houston International Airport; Burma's minister of education was denied a meal in a Columbus, Ohio, cafe; and the finance minister of Ghana was turned away from a Howard Johnson's just outside the nation's capital. Secretary Dulles recognized that such displays of racial prejudice undermined U.S. foreign policy in the Third World, and when the Eisenhower administration appealed to the Supreme Court to strike down segregation in public schools, the attorney general's introductory remarks took note of the international implications. Racism, he said, forfeited U.S. influence in the Third World and provided grist for Communist propaganda mills. When the court handed down its *Brown v. Board of Education* decision in 1954, the U.S. Information Agency translated it with unusual dispatch and broadcast it throughout the world.

Still another handicap for the United States in its quest for influence in the Third World was the American intolerance of revolution. Having become a predominant power, the United States viewed revolutions as potent threats to its interests, liberal political principles, and evolutionary, constitutional procedures. The U.S. government opposed most major twentieth-century revolutions: those in Mexico, China, Russia, Cuba, Vietnam, Iran, and Nicaragua. The United States has preferred the stability and order that seemed to ensure its own prosperity and security. Unable to accommodate revolution, the United States put further distance between itself and the Third World.

Vietnam became for American leaders the spot where the cold war and the Third World converged—where Soviet/Communist expansion seemed to join Third World revolutionary nationalism as a mortal threat to a peaceful world. The Vietnam War, Americanized in the 1960s, became a test of containment. That it was at first fundamentally a Third World struggle for independence against the French and then against the Americans, and that it evolved into a civil war among Vietnamese, should not be overlooked today, but policymakers downplayed such points then. For them, Vietnam represented another front in the cold war: to fail there would be to send a signal that the United States was retreating from its global responsibility as sentinel at the gate.

U.S. decisionmakers rejected warnings from critics, including Senator Aiken, that the Vietnamese were ardent nationalists who would fight tenaciously for nationhood; that the environment of thick forests, tall grasses, and isolated villages was hostile to outsiders; and that the U.S.-backed Saigon government was so corrupt, self-serving, unstable, and unpopular that it could not effectively prosecute a war. Washington's civilian and military leaders stiff-armed negotiations, believing that superior military power would overwhelm the Vietcong and North Vietnamese. As Aiken and many others sensed, Vietnam was an unwinnable war that was depriving the United States of precious resources and youth (the average age of a soldier in Vietnam was nineteen years). In the most general sense, the Vietnam War was undermining U.S. national security.

As more troops and more bombs failed to blunt the attack of Vietnamese adversaries, an intense debate divided Americans at home. Some critics questioned the way the United States was waging war: search-and-destroy missions, B-52 bombing raids, the torching of peasant villages, chemical defoliants like Agent Orange, napalm—these were the tactics of a war of attrition that killed hundreds of thousands and ripped apart the very place the United States said it was trying to save. One U.S. official later admitted that "it was as if we were trying to build a house with a bulldozer and a wrecking crane."9 Some critics thought such methods were unbefitting to America; growing numbers of citizens, watching the carnage on their nightly news, found the war repulsive.

Other critics pointed to the negative domestic effects of the war. It derailed Johnson's Great Society reforms and the civil rights movement. The economic costs also mounted: huge budget deficits and inflation grew from the $2 billion a month spent on the war. Economists also spoke of "opportunity costs": dollars spent on the war and defense could not be spent at home, thus squandering opportunities to improve the U.S. infrastructure. The credibility gap, moreover, revealed that many citizens came to believe that their government officials were liars. Cynicism toward politics and politicians flourished, fed all the more by the Watergate scandal of the early 1970s. Watergate had its origins in part in the Vietnam War; the White House "plumbers" group was created to plug leaks about Nixon's war policy, and the break-ins were designed to silence critics of the war. Vietnam corrupted U.S. politics and endangered civil liberties. Some Americans decried a presidential usurpation of power. The presidents never went to Congress for a declaration of war, and they concealed information essential to good lawmaking—as Johnson did during consideration of the Tonkin Gulf resolution in 1964.

Still other dissenters examined the flaws in the containment doctrine, which did not distinguish vital from peripheral interests or areas, and which did not take account of the indigenous—as distinct from cold war—sources of rebellion. Too often U.S. policymakers believed that Communists, as outside agitators, touched off Third World flash points. "Yet to blame the danger of these [explosions] on the presence of Communists," one scholar has reminded us, "is like blaming the inherent danger in a huge mass of exposed combustible materials on the possible presence of arsonists."[10] Apparently thinking that U.S. power was limitless ("we will bear any burden and pay any price," President John F. Kennedy once proclaimed) policymakers also failed to calculate the strain placed upon the United States by its unrelenting global watch. National security analysts identified the detrimental consequences of the Vietnam War in the alienation of NATO allies and Third World nations and in delaying Soviet-U.S. détente.

A majority of Americans, encouraged by Senator Aiken, came to believe that the United States should withdraw from the war and that entry in the first place had been a mistake. As General Maxwell Taylor observed, America could not win the war because, first, "we didn't know our ally. Secondly, we knew even less about the enemy. And, the last, most inexcusable of our mistakes, was not knowing our own people."[11] What he observed in this last point was that in the agonizing end democracy worked as it should work: a majority of citizens told leaders that they must reverse course, and, however haltingly, they did. Senator Aiken helped this system work.

Cold war, Third World, Vietnam—all three cost the United States dearly and contributed to its relative decline as a great power in the 1970s, the last era of the Aiken Senate years. As one wit put it, "Rome fell; Babylon fell; Scarsdale's turn will come."[12] The sources of this decline, the effects of which we feel this very day, were located first in the exceptional expense of the cold war in dollars. The second source of decline was the challenge to U.S. leadership from members of its own sphere of influence—France and its breakaway from NATO, for example, and Fidel Castro's Cuba and its ouster of U.S. interests from the Caribbean island. And the third source, as I have already discussed, was the emergence of the Third World, which brought new players into the international game. These three elements combined to weaken the standing of the United States in the international system.

Let me emphasize the first source, the economic burden that the cold war, including the Vietnam War, inflicted upon the United States. The costs of maintaining and expanding U.S. global interests climbed steadily: $12.4 billion for the Marshall Plan, $69.5 billion for the Korean War, $22.3 billion for the Alliance for Progress, $172.2 billion for the Vietnam War. For the years 1946–1987, the United States dispensed more than $382 billion in economic and military foreign aid, and international organizations in which the United States was prominent, such as the World Bank, offered $273 billion in assistance. The United States also spent heavily on CIA operations, U.S. Information Agency programs, and support for factions in civil wars. Security links stretched across the globe: from the Rio Pact in Latin America to the Southeast Asia Treaty Organization. In 1959, 1 million Americans were stationed overseas, and the number was only slightly less in 1970.[13]

The alliance building, military expansion, clandestine operations, and interventions, when combined with the creation of a huge nuclear arsenal, meant galloping defense budgets that over the decades have amounted to trillions of dollars. Whereas U.S. military spending stood at $13.5 billion in 1949, it averaged $40 billion in the 1950s, rose to $54 billion in 1960 and $90 billion in 1970, then soared to $155 billion in 1980. By 1988 the military budget had reached more than $300 billion. In the mid-1980s the Defense Department was spending an average of $28 million an hour, twenty-four hours a day, seven days a week.

The massive military spending stabbed at the economy and weakened the U.S. infrastructure. Persistent deficit spending by the federal government drove up the federal debt, which stood at $257 billion in 1950 but by 1986 had reached a staggering $2.1 trillion. In 1986 alone 19 percent of the federal budget disappeared just to pay the interest on the debt. That year, too, 28 percent of the budget was gobbled up by defense. By comparison, 11 percent of federal expenditures went to health and Medicare, 3 percent to education, and 1 percent to environmental programs. In contrast, Japan and West Germany, surging economic competitors, invested in economic development, not in the military.

Military spending constantly drew funds away from other categories so essential to the overall well-being of the nation. Defense spending became "Keynesianism on steroids": in the short term the effect was stimulating, but in the long run the effect was addictive and disastrous.[14] Domestic troubles mounted; lower productivity, a falling savings rate, an inadequately skilled labor force, and weak conservation programs left the U.S. economy vulnerable to sharp swings in prices of imported raw materials, urban decay, a high teenage dropout rate in schools, and lagging investments in research and development.

The United States also became a debtor nation with a serious trade deficit. In 1971 Senator Aiken and other leaders witnessed the first trade deficit since 1888. Although the U.S. economy during the cold war grew in absolute numbers, the U.S. share of the world's material resources decreased relative to other nations. The signs of decline became very evident. The U.S. portion of world gross national product diminished; the U.S. economic growth rate fell behind its competitors. American slippage could also be read in a shrinking share of world exports, a smaller share of world industrial production, and a slumping productivity growth rate.

American leaders of all political persuasions, year after year, decried the detrimental effects of the cold war on the nation's economic health. In the 1950s, for example, President Dwight D. Eisenhower pinpointed the downside to large military expenditures: a federal budget that neglected the domestic infrastructure weakened the nation and thus undercut its military effectiveness. A strong economy, not merely large armed forces and sophisticated nuclear equipment, he argued, was essential to defense. Strong nations required a well-educated, healthy citizenry and work force. "Every gun that is made, every warship launched, every rocket fired signifies ... a theft from those who hunger and are not fed," the Republican president said in 1953. He went on: "The cost of one modern heavy bomber is this: a modern brick school in more than thirty cities." He, like us today, found the "peace dividend" elusive.

Senator Aiken sensed the relationship between military spending and U.S. decline even if he could not grasp its full dimensions or implications in the early 1970s. He noted in 1972, for example, that Great Britain's entry into the Common Market might hurt the U.S. international trade position and send the United States further into debt because of an adverse balance of payments. That year, too, he bemoaned the federal debt's having reached $450 billion and senators' general silence on defense appropriations. A year later he worried about the growing economic competition posed by Japan and West Germany and agreed with his close colleague Mike Mansfield that Western Europe should bear more of the cost of its own security.[15]

To highlight the boom in defense spending and the deteriorating American condition is not to imply that the United States, in Aiken's time or in the 1990s, was on its economic knees. Despite its many domestic problems and a steady series of recessions, the United States still ranked (and ranks) as a wealthy, powerful nation with impressive talents and resources compared to other countries. The compelling point is that the cold war was very, very costly, and the United States has suffered decline. Aiken and others did not see a way out of the defense burden, a burden they thought necessary, but they knew the nation was paying large and painful domestic costs for its global foreign policy.

The consequences of the four eras that coincided with Aiken's Senate years became conspicuous after he left Washington. The theme of restoration has been central to the foreign policies of Jimmy Carter, Ronald Reagan, and George Bush. Reagan appealed for a "national reawakening."[16] A core feature of the immediate post–cold war international order is the U.S. attempt to recoup lost influence, reestablish credibility, and reassert superpower status. Bush, too, promised a restoration of U.S. power and prestige, a reestablishment of the nation's hegemony. In a world moving from cold war to hot peace, Bush lifted Theodore Roosevelt's big stick once again to reclaim for the United States the role of global police.

When Bush responded to the Iraqi invasion of Kuwait, he explained that the Gulf War marked the first post–cold war era "test of our mettle": "let no one doubt our staying power."[17] In his

1991 state of the Union address, Bush spoke of the "defining hour" and appealed for national "renewal."[18] "When we prevail," Bush advised, "there will be a renewed credibility for the United States."[19] The Gulf War, it might be suggested, was one way the United States sought to regain the ground the cold war had whittled away.

Some Reagan-Bush officials celebrated the arrival of a unipolar world with the United States prominently at the top. Critics decry such rhetoric and dispute American claims to international supremacy. "Hegemony," the historian Thomas McCormick wrote, "necessarily rests upon both military and economic power, and the dilemma facing a maturing hegemon is that it cannot sustain both."[20] If a major power spends heavily on its military, it hurts its domestic economy; if it bleeds its economy, it is less able to sustain a competitive global position. Yet if it reduces its defense spending to attend to domestic priorities, it endangers its global status, which derives in good part from military superiority. The United States in the 1990s faces this classic dilemma.

Although it has become fashionable to say that the United States won the cold war, and it is clear that democratization and free-market capitalism are ascending, in fact the cold war had no winners. Both the United States and the Soviet Union spent themselves into weakened conditions; both lost major wars in the Third World. Both paid tremendous prices for waging the cold war. It may be too strong to suggest, as foreign affairs analyst Marshall Shulman has, that the overmilitarized United States and the former states of the Soviet Union are now like "dinosaurs that face if not extinction, at least perilous futures."[21] Senator George Aiken often peered into perilous futures—into World War II, the cold war, the challenge of the Third World, the Vietnam War, and the decline of U.S. power in the 1970s—and he probably saw more clearly than most observers.

Aiken and J. William Fulbright in the Senate Foreign Relations Committee, 1970. Courtesy of Bailey/Howe Library, University of Vermont.

7

The "Wise Old Owl": George D. Aiken and Foreign Affairs, 1941–1975

Mark A. Stoler

*D*URING HIS THIRTY-FOUR YEARS IN THE U.S. Senate, George D. Aiken won enormous respect and admiration for his independence, honesty, dry wit, and commonsense wisdom. He exhibited these characteristics in numerous areas, but they were most noticed and publicized in the realm of foreign affairs—especially in regard to the Vietnam War during the 1960s. Labeled the leading Republican "dove" on the Senate Foreign Relations Committee during those tumultuous years, he achieved great notoriety for supposedly suggesting in 1966 that President Lyndon B. Johnson end the conflict simply by declaring a victory and getting out.

Behind this fame as a war critic, however, lay some apparent inconsistencies. Although he attacked administration policies in

Vietnam and abuses of executive power, Aiken simultaneously supported all military appropriations for the war, insisted that the United States had a commitment to South Vietnam, and opposed Senate efforts to set a timetable for withdrawal. Many Johnson supporters therefore praised Aiken's defense of administration policies, whereas Johnson's critics hailed Aiken's stand in the Senate.

These apparent inconsistencies are understandable only if one realizes that Aiken's public position on Vietnam bore little resemblance to his real beliefs. He never stated that Johnson should declare a victory and get out, and he did not consider himself a dove on the war. Furthermore, Southeast Asia was not an area he deemed very important to the United States or one he even knew much about. Indeed—and it is ironic in light of his later fame—foreign affairs were never his highest interest and was not a major concern for him before the 1960s.

Aiken concentrated primarily on domestic issues, above all the problems of American agriculture, especially those of the small farmer within his home state of Vermont. Although he entered the Senate in 1940, he neither requested nor received appointment to the Foreign Relations Committee until 1954. His early years in the Senate, however, coincided with the full emergence of the United States as an international actor, first in World War II and then in the cold war. The United States' new global standing would control domestic as well as international politics throughout Aiken's Senate career and force him not only to focus on foreign affairs but also to recognize the inseparability of foreign relations from his domestic concerns.

Aiken's education in the importance of foreign affairs began even before he entered the Senate. The 1939 movement to nominate him for president faltered in part because of his lack of foreign policy interest or expertise as World War II came to dominate political debate.[1] His first major Senate speech in 1941 concerned lend-lease aid to Britain.[2] Although he opposed this measure, he was by no means an isolationist, and by war's end he was championing a strong international role for the United States in the postwar world.

Aiken had concluded that the long-term problem of agricultural surplus could be solved only through a federally directed expansion of foreign markets undertaken in coordination with an internationalist foreign policy to feed the world's hungry. More specifically, the St. Lawrence Seaway, his pet project to provide Vermont dairy farmers with cheap electricity and feed grains, had been stymied for many years by stumbling blocks in negotiations with Canada and domestic opposition within the Senate and its Foreign Relations Committee.

In 1954 Aiken gave up thirteen years' seniority on the Senate Labor Committee to obtain a seat on the Foreign Relations Committee.[3] In that same year he helped obtain Senate passage of the long-delayed St. Lawrence project as well as a program for overseas agricultural sales, the so-called food for peace bill (PL 480) that enabled the federal government to sell U.S. agricultural surplus abroad in return for local currencies.[4] Throughout the rest of the decade, he continued to focus on issues of agricultural trade and aid, as well as hemispheric relations and the United Nations.

Aiken's emerging views on foreign policy in general reflected this strong concern with agriculture and the beliefs he had developed earlier as a rural Progressive in Vermont politics. Echoing in simple language the basic ideas of American thinkers from Thomas Jefferson and James Madison to Reinhold Niebuhr, Aiken considered the "urge to monopoly," to control resources and peoples, a human instinct that inevitably led to tyranny if it was not checked. As governor of Vermont he had fought this instinct, whether it was exhibited by powerful utility companies in alliance with conservative Republicans or by Franklin Roosevelt's New Deal in trying to increase federal power at local expense. In international affairs Aiken saw the same instinct at work in the actions of dictators, multinational corporations, European colonialists attempting to maintain their overseas possessions amid a rising tide of Third World revolution, and Communists who despite their egalitarian rhetoric were no different from other tyrants.

The United States had to use its power to check these Communists, Aiken maintained, but not at the risk of losing its own liberty in the process. Success in such a venture required an emphasis on economic aid rather than military action overseas. It also required a clear awareness of the true nature of communism and the world situation and a recognition that there were indeed limits to what appeared to be the United States' unlimited power.

Aiken's insistence on the superiority of economic over military means was based on his belief that communism, like all other tyrannies, fed on hunger and despair. It could therefore be fought most effectively by raising world living standards through exporting surplus American food and increasing international trade. This economic approach would also help small Communist countries break out of the Soviet orbit, for the nationalism within those states was inherently hostile to Soviet domination and required only a little U.S. support, as witnessed in Yugoslavia.[5]

Military means, in contrast, Aiken considered both ineffective and dangerous. To use them meant risking not only a nuclear confrontation with the Soviets but also the destruction of liberty at home, for war inevitably led to national financial impoverishment and greatly expanded executive power. Throughout his years as governor of Vermont in the 1930s, Aiken warned against the threat to liberty posed by Roosevelt's enormous expansion of executive power. He continued to do so in the Senate. Indeed, he opposed the 1941 Lend-Lease Bill not because it provided aid to Britain, which he favored, but because it gave the president too much discretionary power.[6] A decade later his opposition to expansion of the Korean conflict was based in part on similar grounds, and during the 1950s he cosponsored the Bricker amendment to limit presidential power in foreign affairs.[7] At the same time he supported a strong United Nations to prevent international disputes from leading to nuclear confrontation.

It is clear that Aiken considered communism a global menace, feared both Soviet and Chinese expansion, and at first agreed with President Eisenhower's domino theory as applied to Asia and the Pacific. He did not, however, believe in a monolithic conspiracy directed from Moscow and responsible for all the world's troubles.[8] The real cause of global unrest, he argued, was the monopoly on land, a situation that invited rebellion and one the United States could not hope to control despite its extensive power. "We cannot order the world to our liking," he warned as early as 1960, and realistic limitations should therefore be placed on U.S. ambitions overseas. Using an economic and geographic standard, he concluded that the country's interests and power were greatest in the Western Hemisphere and gradually decreased the greater the distance from American shores. U.S. efforts should therefore concentrate on Canada and Latin America, and elsewhere the United States should count on allies and Communist-nationalist incompatibility (most notably the emerging Sino-Soviet split) to block monopolistic forces.[9]

Such beliefs did not weaken Aiken's high status within his Republican party or with its Democratic opposition. To the contrary, he quickly developed a reputation for bipartisanship and reasonableness that led to his retention as chair of the Canadian subcommittee long after his party had lost its Senate majority, and to efforts by the Kennedy and Johnson administrations to obtain his support during the 1960s. To an extent this may have resulted from a perception that Aiken felt "not altogether happy with his party" because of a lack of federal projects in Vermont during the Eisenhower years and that "with a little encouragement," according to one Kennedy aide, he "could prove to be a very friendly Republican."[10]

Equally if not more important were the degree of compatibility that appeared to exist between Aiken and the Democratic presidents and the odd Republican seniority situation on the Foreign Relations Committee. Although Aiken was the senior Republican on the committee, his late entry in 1954 meant that he was not the ranking Republican. That position belonged to Bourke Hickenlooper of Iowa, a conservative who disagreed with Democratic policies far more frequently than Aiken did. Kennedy therefore turned to Aiken in an attempt to win moderate Republican support for his policies, meeting with him privately after the 1961 Bay of Pigs fiasco and inviting him to Moscow for the signing of the Nuclear Test Ban Treaty in 1963.

Aiken's backing of administration foreign policies quickly faltered, however, as Kennedy and Johnson tended to act aggressively in international affairs without consulting Congress. Nowhere was this inclination more apparent than in the issue of the Vietnam conflict, and on no policy did Aiken assert his disagreement more forcefully. Indeed, the militarization and escalation of U.S. involvement in Vietnam during the 1960s violated most of Aiken's beliefs and led him into the role of dissenter for which he became so famous.

The content of Aiken's dissent also revealed the enormous impact on his thinking of an earlier U.S. military involvement in Asia, the intervention in Korea, which had resulted in an unwinnable ground war, the possibility of nuclear conflict, a loss of Allied support, increased executive power, an end to bipartisan foreign policy, and the McCarthy-era search for scapegoats. Aiken had originally supported Truman's decision to send troops to Korea on the grounds that North Korea was the aggressor and that the U.S. response to this challenge would have worldwide repercussions. Yet he complained that Truman's actions and lack of prior consultation with Congress had left little alternative save to stand by the president and hope he was correct. When China intervened it became apparent that Truman had miscalculated the depth of the Chinese commitment to North Korea. Breaking with many of his Republican colleagues, Aiken opposed expanding the conflict because he believed the United States could not win a ground war in Asia, the nationalists in Taiwan could not defeat the Chinese Communists, and nuclear warfare was out of the question unless the United States was prepared to fight most of the world. At the same time Aiken blasted the Truman administration for its blundering and usurpation of power, and he warned that the internal menace posed by continuation of the war was just as dangerous as military defeat. In 1952 he strongly supported Eisenhower's presidential candidacy on the grounds that only he could end the conflict.[11]

Aiken's dissent regarding the Vietnam War a decade later was also heavily influenced by his close friendship with Mike Mansfield, the Democratic Senate majority leader. It was Mansfield, in fact, who labeled Aiken a "wise old owl," rather than a hawk or dove, for his statements on the war.[12] Those statements often reflected the ideas of Mansfield, who was known as an Asia expert and who breakfasted with Aiken every morning.[13]

Aiken saw Vietnam as an unwinnable war. The Vietcong, an indigenous army rather than a part of any "outside aggression," could match any U.S. troop buildup. Commitment of U.S. forces would thus be unsuccessful. It would also Americanize a civil conflict and destroy both the independence of the Saigon government and the national self-determination the United States was supposedly defending. Furthermore, bombing North Vietnam would increase, not decrease, the flow of aid to the Vietcong, forcing Hanoi into greater reliance on its traditional enemy, China. U.S. intervention would thereby weld Communist nations together at the very moment competing nationalisms had begun separating them. As in Korea, Chinese entry into the conflict would mean a full-scale land war that the United States could win only with nuclear weapons.

Even if China did not intervene, the extensive U.S. military commitment to South Vietnam was tying down American strength in a relatively unimportant area, thereby decreasing U.S. influence in more important regions and giving the Soviet Union substantial victories without cost. "I do not believe that if the Soviet Union and the Chinese worked hard in trying to find a location for a showdown," Aiken stated in 1966, "they could have found one more disadvantageous to us than in Southeast Asia."[14] The domestic consequences of the massive U.S. military commitment by that year were even worse—high casualties, a weakened economy, a divided populace, an end to bipartisanship in foreign policy, and a dangerous extension of executive power. By 1967 Aiken was referring to the war as a "debacle" that reminded him of the ancient Romans—"so concerned with their own world prestige that they forgot what was going on at home."[15]

At the same time, however, Aiken consistently maintained that the United States had a definite albeit limited commitment to South Vietnam based upon its responsibility for having helped to transport hundreds of thousands of refugees from the north after the 1954 Geneva accords. A continued U.S. presence in the south was mandatory, he repeatedly stated, in order to protect the South Vietnamese from a massacre and block Chinese expansion.

Aiken's stand on presidential versus congressional power revealed a similar duality. Although a strong critic of executive power, Aiken insisted that only the president had the authority and ability to conduct day-to-day foreign and military policy. The proper role of Congress was to discuss and state overall policy objectives, appropriate funds, and advise on projected major actions. If the president sought this advice and kept Congress informed, then that body should agree to his daily conduct of affairs.[16]

President Dwight D. Eisenhower had done just that, according to Aiken. After consulting with congressional leaders, he had rejected an unlimited military commitment in 1954 in favor of a more limited commitment to South Vietnam, which Aiken strongly supported. But his Democratic successor had *not* sought congressional advice and had unilaterally expanded the commitment while providing Congress with optimistic reports Aiken found to be at "complete variance with the facts." By 1963 Kennedy had also helped in overthrowing South Vietnamese president Ngo Dinh Diem, a man Aiken greatly admired.[17] After Kennedy's assassination, President Johnson attempted to heal this growing rift through extensive consultation with Aiken and other congressional leaders. Johnson consistently rejected the Vermonter's advice on Vietnam, however, and gradually substituted briefing sessions for true consultation. Furthermore, his day-to-day conduct of affairs was so manipulative that by mid-1965 he had created a new policy of virtually unlimited military commitment without congressional approval. This Aiken considered an unconstitutional abuse of executive power.[18] Johnson did fulfill the letter, if not the spirit, of "consultation." But as with Truman's handling of Korea, Congress could only back Johnson's unilateral commitments and hope the president's actions made sense.

The full scope of this dilemma became apparent to Aiken during the August 1964 Tonkin Gulf crisis. In response to two supposed North Vietnamese attacks on U.S. destroyers in the Tonkin Gulf, Johnson ordered retaliatory air strikes against North Vietnamese bases. He also requested and received a congressional resolution supporting his actions, which he would later use to justify sending more than 500,000 men to Vietnam without any declaration of war. As numerous scholars have noted, and as the Foreign Relations Committee discovered four years later, the entire episode was tainted with duplicity and manipulation. The North Vietnamese attacks were actually responses to clandestine U.S.–South Vietnamese raids along the North Vietnamese coast (called OPLAN 34A by the White House staff) as well as intelligence-gathering operations (DeSoto), and what the White House claimed was the second attack probably never took place. Furthermore, the administration had been preparing the congressional resolution for months beforehand and had written it in such a way as to obtain, as one administration official stated, "the full support of the school of thought headed by Senator Mansfield and Senator Aiken" so as to leave only "die-hard opposition from Senator [Wayne] Morse [D–Ore.] and his very few cohorts."[19] On the evening of August 4, President Johnson called Aiken, Mansfield, and other congressional leaders to the White House. In his memoirs he stated that by meeting's end, each legislator had "expressed his wholehearted endorsement of our course of action and of the proposed resolution."[20]

Johnson's own files reveal that this was overstatement at best. Although unaware of all the facts in the situation, Mansfield and Aiken knew enough from previous Foreign Relations Committee and White House briefings to voice dissent. Mansfield read a memorandum at the evening meeting opposing retaliation. Aiken reinforced him by warning of possible Chinese intervention and questioned the administration's version of events by pointedly asking CIA director John J. McCone for information on the "provocation, if any," for the second North Vietnamese attack. Johnson, however, had made up his mind, and the dissenting congressional leaders quickly realized there was no way they could effectively oppose his resolution or stop him from using his power, as commander in chief, to retaliate. As Aiken bitterly noted at the end of the meeting, "By the time you send it up [to Congress], there won't be anything for us to do but support you."[21] Despite "grave misgivings" over the wisdom of Johnson's actions, he consequently voted for the Tonkin Gulf resolution and military appropriations, on the grounds that Congress could not oppose the president for exercising his constitutional powers.[22] He made clear, however, that his votes were in no way to be interpreted as his approval of administration actions or continued executive war without prior congressional debate and consent.[23]

Aiken's way out of these dualities on the war and executive power was to recommend that Johnson take the Vietnam conflict to the United Nations Security Council for mediation. But by 1966 he was aware that such a move would not work. Seeing both its major enemies preoccupied in Southeast Asia, the Soviet Union would block any settlement. Furthermore, the Johnson administration continued to ignore Aiken's advice and exhibited what he called an "almost overpowering phobia ... toward ideas emanating from Congress." By February 1966 Aiken was forced to admit that getting out of Vietnam while ensuring self-determination for the area would take a "near miracle," a situation he blamed as much on Soviet cynicism as Johnson's obstinance.[24]

Aiken's efforts to overcome these obstacles would lead to his most famous comments about Vietnam. In 1965 he and Mansfield launched a joint attack against calls for escalation emanating from the administration and from Republican hawks in Congress, most notably Gerald Ford (R–Mich.) and Melvin Laird (R–Wis.). Such coordination enabled both men to overcome their delicate political positions. As Senate majority leader, Mansfield could not publicly criticize the president and was forced to limit his dissent to long, confidential letters to Johnson ending with strong reassertions of his continued loyalty. As a leading Republican, however,

Aiken could openly denounce presidential policy and state in stronger language what Mansfield was saying privately. On the other side, within his party, Aiken could go no further than to state that he was "somewhat disturbed" by hawkish statements, whereas Mansfield could of course use harsher language against the Republican hawks. Each could then use milder statements and leading questions as well as words of support on the floor of the Senate to aid the other.[25]

Predating Senator J. William Fulbright's famous public break with Johnson, this bipartisan critique by two of the most respected members of the Senate could not be dismissed as merely the ravings of a single disgruntled senator or as partisan politics. Indeed, it seemed to have an effect on President Johnson, who by late 1965 had stated his willingness to negotiate directly with Hanoi and accept UN help, suspended the bombing of North Vietnam, and asked Mansfield to lead a special Senate delegation on a worldwide trip to explore the possibilities of a negotiated peace. Aiken was selected as the ranking Republican on this mission and coauthored the highly publicized report warning that the United States faced either an open-ended and unwinnable military confrontation in Vietnam or a negotiated settlement that in all likelihood would not guarantee U.S. goals in the area.[26]

Johnson was polite and proper,[27] but he refused to heed the Aiken-Mansfield advice and in early 1966 resumed the bombing of North Vietnam. Aiken responded by taking his message to the people via the televised Foreign Relations Committee hearings of 1966. Although his statements during those hearings were minimal, his questions were probing and at points devastating. Administration officials were forced to admit in response to those queries that the Vietcong constituted an indigenous force rather than a northern invasion, that they financed their effort in part through receipt of "protection money" from U.S. corporations operating in the south, and that continuation of the war could make the United States as totalitarian as the communism it was supposedly fighting.[28]

Yet Aiken continued to vote for military appropriations on

the grounds that the president was exercising his constitutional authority, that the United States had a definite commitment to South Vietnam, and that dividing a nation on the brink of full-scale war was "unthinkable." With Johnson rejecting his advice, the "most" left to him was "the hope that the President is right and that I have been wrong."29 His pessimism only increased during the ensuing months. "If we can get out of Vietnam with the respect of the world and still ensure South Vietnam will be left for the South Vietnamese," he stated on February 21, "it would be a near miracle."30 Such a miracle was not forthcoming. Instead of ending the bombing of North Vietnam, Johnson expanded the number of targets in the north and stopped even the briefing sessions with members of the Foreign Relations Committee.31

On October 19, 1966, just before the start of a major strategy conference in Manila, Aiken made one final attempt to influence the president as well as solve the contradictions in his own position by suggesting a novel way to begin negotiations. The real goal of the U.S. military buildup, he argued, had been not the stated and fraudulent as well as unobtainable objective of stopping "outside aggression" by Hanoi but merely rescuing U.S. troops that had been in "clear and present danger of military defeat." Johnson's escalation had accomplished this goal. He could thus declare a "victory," begin a "gradual redeployment" of U.S. forces around "strategic centers," and substitute "intensive reconnaissance" for bombing. This was in no way equivalent to a precipitate or even phased withdrawal, Aiken emphasized. U.S. forces would have to remain in Vietnam "for some time." But the combination of redeployment with cessation of bombing and a declaration of victory would remove the issue of "face" or "credibility" as a factor precluding negotiations, force the burden of further escalation onto the enemy, and open the door to a resumption of the "political warfare" that had properly characterized the early U.S. involvement in Vietnam.32

"Senator Aiken must be joking," quipped the *Burlington Free Press*.33 He wasn't. Nor was his idea completely original. As Senator Frank Lausche (D–Ohio) and numerous newspapers noted, Aiken was essentially calling for a shift to the "enclave" strategy enunciated earlier in the year by retired General James Gavin, but with the novel addition of the "victory" statement so as to provide a de-escalation of objectives to match the strategic de-escalation Gavin had recommended as well as a face-saving device for the president and the nation. "It may be a far-fetched proposal," Aiken admitted, "but nothing else has worked." With support from Mansfield and Fulbright as well as extensive press coverage, Aiken became famous for a classic example of Yankee wit and wisdom.[34]

In the ensuing months Aiken pushed his "formula" while stressing that U.S. forces would have to remain in Vietnam for at least fifteen years and perhaps to the end of the century. Total withdrawal, he insisted, was just as unrealistic as total victory.[35] But the administration continued to ignore him, and in mid-1967 he bitterly commented that he had no more advice for the White House. "They would not take it if I gave it," he stated on the Senate floor, "so why waste my breath?" In the short run, he was forced to admit, there was nothing further he could do. Voting against military appropriations with half a million men in the field and nuclear confrontation a possibility was to him unthinkable.[36]

But to cover the long run, Aiken began to press two related campaigns: one to defeat Johnson in the 1968 elections and the other to reassert congressional power to define U.S. foreign policy. The administration, he now began to emphasize, was too bound by its own preconceptions ever to make peace or give U.S. policy the "fresh appraisal" it so desperately needed. Such a "new look" in Asia should be the Republican promise for 1968. Not only would it lead to victory and peace, but it would also mend the hawk-dove split within the Republican party (which had surfaced in May 1967 with the publication of a dovish Republican policy committee report on Vietnam and an immediate hawkish counterattack)—much the same way Eisenhower had closed the rift in 1952.[37]

Aiken also linked his lack of faith in the Johnson administration to revival of congressional power by suggesting that the Senate debate the "basic question" of whether U.S. national interests required military forces on the Asian mainland. Such a discussion, he maintained, was part of the constitutional responsibility of Congress to formulate foreign policy, a responsibility it had "almost totally abdicated during the past decade."38 At the same time Aiken renewed his call for a U.S. initiative in the United Nations not because he thought it would work but because it would show the world the Soviet Union's part in continuing the war and would begin to reestablish congressional definition of U.S. policy. In October 1967 he and Mansfield cosponsored a "sense of the Senate" resolution requesting the president to submit the Vietnam conflict to the Security Council.39

When the administration responded by questioning the loyalty of Senate dissenters, Aiken pointed to his voting record for war funds and accused the White House of attempting to make Congress a scapegoat for its own mistakes. It had become "the prisoner of its own bad rhetoric" in its attempts to justify the stupidity or lack of imagination involved in fighting nationalists first and Communists incidentally in Vietnam. The monolithic Communist conspiracy he now bluntly labeled a "myth," an "act of invention," and a "self-destructive fantasy." Political negotiations begun via his 1966 formula still constituted the best alternative, though he warned that this was only a first step and that U.S. forces would have to remain in Vietnam "for some time."40

Aiken reiterated these beliefs after the stunning Tet offensive of early 1968 and Johnson's subsequent decisions to halt bombing, begin peace talks, and not seek reelection. By year's end Aiken had also concluded that the peace talks would not succeed and had returned to the idea, originally expressed as a hope in early 1966, that the war would gradually fade away as the U.S. withdrew its forces and bolstered the Saigon government. Newly elected Republican President Richard M. Nixon's plans for phased withdrawal and "Vietnamization" were in complete accord with such thinking, and Aiken therefore gave him substantial support. Precipitate withdrawal, he warned, would lead to chaos in South Vietnam, a massacre of U.S. supporters, and a new McCarthy era at home as people searched for scapegoats. The past could not simply be undone. Southeast Asia, he ruefully stated, "is, and will remain, an important area of national security if only because we foolishly made it so."[41]

Aiken also maintained that the complex specifics of gradual withdrawal were the president's proper responsibility. The function of Congress was to define, not execute, U.S. policy. Aiken therefore urged his colleagues to cease criticizing Nixon's actions and instead regain their constitutional role by redefining U.S. policy in light of the Vietnam experience. Such a redefinition should overthrow the "New Deal" concepts and methods of the past thirty-five years, which he felt had led to Vietnam, and replace them with a realistic understanding of the limits of U.S. power, new machinery for execution, and legislative-executive as well as interparty cooperation.[42]

In line with such thinking, Aiken consistently defended Nixon against his Senate detractors. He did oppose the Cambodian and Laotian invasions of 1970–1971 but in relatively mild terms, defending the constitutionality of the president's use of force. He attacked Senate timetables for withdrawal as abuses of legislative power, supported the 1972 bombing of the north, constantly reminded his colleagues of the steadily decreasing number of U.S. troops and deaths in Vietnam, and sarcastically implied that their "conversion" to his 1966 ideas was motivated by partisan politics. Why, he asked, had so many of these Democratic dissenters begun to champion his views only when a Republican took over the White House?[43]

Unlike his experience during the 1960s, in the early 1970s Aiken saw significant executive action in support of his ideas. The entire Nixon-Kissinger "grand design"—including the Nixon Doctrine emphasizing the use of indigenous rather than U.S. forces in the Pacific, the startling presidential visit to and recognition of Communist China, the détente with the Soviet Union, the 1973 Paris peace accords, and final withdrawal of U.S. forces from Vietnam—were all in line with recommendations he had made. But instead of a healthy Saigon government or a new era of executive-congressional cooperation and bipartisanship in foreign affairs, Aiken witnessed a steadily worsening situation in both Vietnam and Washington that culminated during 1974–1975 in the fall of Saigon—and of Nixon.

Efforts to categorize George Aiken's positions in foreign affairs founder on the seemingly contradictory nature of his general as well as specific beliefs. Some historians would define him as an economic-open-door Wilsonian for his advocacy of expanded overseas markets as a means of promoting American values abroad while relieving domestic problems of surplus production. Yet this worldview was tempered by what has historically been its opposite—a realistic assessment of the limits of U.S. power and the true nature of world politics. Similarly, his opposition to the Vietnam War and to increased executive power was tempered by his views regarding the continued U.S. commitment to South Vietnam and the proper powers of the presidency.

Trying to evaluate what Aiken accomplished in foreign affairs is equally frustrating. On the surface it would seem he achieved nothing, for his advice was ignored by the White House and by most of his colleagues and his hopes were dashed again and again. It is ironic that he appeared to have won fame and notoriety for something he never said and for a position he never held, over an issue he tried unsuccessfully to keep unimportant.

We must look, however, at what did not happen as well as what did. Johnson did not escalate the Vietnam conflict to the point of bringing China into the war, for example, and the hawks did not gain control of the Republican party during the 1960s and early 1970s. Aiken's role in preventing certain occurrences is at once difficult to assess yet obvious. Although his influence and prestige had never been quantifiable, his colleagues all agreed that both were enormous. Without doubt, that prestige and influence led many of those colleagues privately to rethink their views when Aiken voiced his opposition to the administration's policies. That opposition in turn brought respectability and bipartisanship to the antiwar movement at an early date. His influence was also apparent in the 1968 Republican position on the war and in Nixon's overall foreign policy. Perhaps most fittingly, his views were reflected in the 1973 Paris peace accords. As numerous commentators have noted, everyone at Paris appeared to have accepted a modified version of the "Aiken formula": while the United States continued to withdraw, all parties to the agreement simultaneously declared a victory.

Luncheon honoring the Canadian delegation to the Canada–U.S. Interparliamentary Group meeting, Old Supreme Court Chamber, April 21, 1960. Left to right: Aiken, chair of the U.S. Senate Delegation; Mark Drouin, Speaker of the Canadian Senate; Roland Michener, Speaker of the Canadian House of Commons; Edna F. Kelly, chair of the U.S. House of Representatives delegation. Courtesy of Bailey/Howe Library, University of Vermont.

8

George Aiken and Canada

Charles F. O'Brien

*I*N JANUARY 1972 THE LONGTIME POLITICAL COM-
mentator for Canada's Southam news service, Charles
Lynch, wrote a tongue-in-cheek piece for the *Toronto Star* in
which he urged Canadians to get to know their "congressman": "If
you live in Quebec," wrote Lynch, "your Congressman is Sen.
George Aiken. He reads Hansard daily and has complained that
Nixon's economic policies would cripple Canada."[1]

At the Aiken Legacy Conference held at the University of
Vermont in 1991, University of Toronto history professor Robert
Bothwell remarked that early in his presidency, Harry Truman,
despite having only a rudimentary knowledge of Canada, had
accurately identified the two countries' "sense of community."[2]
This important aspect of Canadian-U.S. relations gets too little
attention. Along the northern border of the United States,
Canada's national anthem is often played at sporting events—even
when there is no Canadian participant—and American Legion
posts from Maine to Washington routinely fly the Maple Leaf.
Such signs of community are common for the length of the long

border. There are hundreds of agreements between our two countries that will never make an Associated Press or Southam wire. These usually involve mutual aid of one form or another between fire departments, rescue squads, game wardens, and so on. For the millions of Canadian and U.S. citizens who live within an hour's drive of the border (including almost 200,000 Vermonters, or almost 40 percent of the state's population), this sense of community is seldom noticed simply because it is part of the fabric of daily life.

Before he entered politics, Aiken was a nurseryman in Putney, in the southeastern corner of Vermont—about as far from the Canadian border as one can get and still be in Vermont. In fact, Aiken was in public life for a considerable time before he showed much interest in Canada. His book *Speaking from Vermont,* written in 1938, does not contain a single reference to Canada. As governor of Vermont in the 1930s, he showed, with few exceptions, an essentially perfunctory interest in Canada.

The most notable exception was the St. Lawrence Seaway. Aiken was an ardent supporter of the seaway, which he saw as a means to break the railroad monopoly on freight and to bring feed grain from the Midwest to New England at lower rates. He was part of the classic tradition of farm state politicians who viewed the railroads as octopuses. Indeed, there was a powerful current of late-nineteenth-century populism evident throughout Aiken's career. With the seaway, he believed, would come the Champlain Waterway—a short canal linking Lake Champlain to both the seaway system and the high seas. Such a link would be the key to industrial development of the Champlain Valley and would lower grain prices.

Another enduring concern in Aiken's political life was the production of electric power, which brought his local interests into the larger framework of Canadian-U.S. relations. He fought to block dams that would do to his beloved Vermont what the Quabbin Reservoir had done to a huge tract in Massachusetts. Yet the state's economy required more and cheaper power. Ontario Hydro, the St. Lawrence project, and Hydro-Québec all fit perfectly into Aiken's vision of the correct way to develop Vermont. They also required levels of Canadian-U.S. cooperation that were unprecedented until World War II.

Aiken was elected to the U.S. Senate in 1940 and almost immediately became heavily engaged in Canadian-U.S. affairs. His first Senate speech denounced the Lend-Lease Bill (which he termed the "aid to Britain" bill). But he contrasted the folly of compromising U.S. neutrality in Europe with the necessity of defending Canada, noting that he and his constituents "would go all the way, down to the last dollar and the last man, to protect Canada."[3]

Over the course of more than three decades in the Senate, Aiken's two most important committee assignments—Agriculture and Foreign Relations—involved extensive dealings with Canada. As a senator from what was then primarily an agricultural state, Aiken had seized his first opportunity to serve on the Agriculture Committee. A similar route led him to the Foreign Relations Committee. The search for lower-cost feed grain for Vermont farmers and cheaper electrical power for the state's small industrial base made the St. Lawrence Seaway one of his highest priorities, and of course the Foreign Relations Committee was central in securing passage of the seaway bill.

Aiken was the moving spirit behind the establishment of the Canada-U.S. Interparliamentary Group in 1958. But Mitchell Sharp, Canada's minister of external affairs, recalled meeting with Aiken over wheat agreements long before the founding of the group.[4] Aiken had the wisdom to see that Canada and the United States were entering perilous waters. Among the many contentious issues that arose in the decade following 1958 were the positioning of U.S. missiles in Canada; arming those missiles with nuclear warheads; Canada's trade with the People's Republic of China; the Chicago diversion (a plan to draw water from the Great Lakes into the Chicago River in order to help Chicago get rid of its waste); Canada's lack of support during the Cuban missile crisis; the legendary personal antipathy between President

Kennedy and Prime Minister John Diefenbaker; the Vietnam War in its many guises, including the asylum Canada gave to U.S. draft dodgers during the war; difficult auto trade negotiations in the mid-1960s; the defiant 1969 voyage of a privately owned U.S. vessel through waters claimed by Canada; and the Alaska pipeline, to which Canada objected from the outset on grounds of likely damage to its shores from oil spills.

There is very little doubt that the Canada-U.S. Interparliamentary Group in general and Aiken in particular operated to mitigate tensions during this difficult period. For example, U.S. pressure on Canada to accept nuclear warheads on missiles positioned within its territory became an issue in the Canadian federal election in 1963. Aiken's response was to put out a press release designed to soothe Canadian feelings: "It seems to me very clear on the basis of our relations with Canada over many years that overt and clumsy efforts on the part of any United States official to influence Canadian policy decisions are likely to achieve results opposite to the ones intended." He also called a meeting of his Subcommittee on Canadian Affairs on February 4, 1963, "to determine whether in fact United States officials have attempted to exercise unwarranted pressure on the Canadian Government and, if so, for what reasons."5

It is also clear that Aiken and the Interparliamentary Group served as one of the key sources of the 1989 free trade agreement between Canada and the United States. In 1962, for example, the group's discussions centered on the consequences for North America of the European Economic Community, especially in light of Britain's possible entry. This discussion, in turn, led to a consideration of freer trade as one response to changing international trading conditions.6 By 1968 freer trade seemed to be assumed; the discussion that year centered on the different impact free trade would have on the two countries.

Aiken's position as the Senate's leading authority on Canada during the 1960s and 1970s is indicated by his tenure as chair of the Subcommittee on Canadian Affairs for most of this period, despite Democratic control of the Senate. It was during this time that Mike Mansfield, majority leader of the Senate and Aiken's close friend, characterized him as an "owl":[7]

> There has been a good deal of reference in the press in late months to the categories of the dove and the hawk.
>
> Personally, I do not pay too much attention to those designations. What I think the Senator from Vermont typifies and personifies, if I may use the word, is the owl. He is the wise man, the man who looks ahead, the man who is unswerving in his support of the United States, but who is also aware of the dangers which confront us in any given situation.[8]

Aiken relinquished the chair in 1969. At the meeting of the Interparliamentary Group that year, Congressman Cornelius Gallagher, a Democrat from New Jersey, said, "Regardless of who sits up here, the guiding spirit and light of the American delegation at all times will be George Aiken."[9] In 1973, two years before his retirement, in the face of some of the difficult issues mentioned above, Aiken once again helped to calm troubled waters. After the Interparliamentary Group's meeting that year, Senator Gale McGee (D–Wyo.), new cochair of the group, wrote to Aiken: "Thanks for getting us headed in the right direction.... I fear our Canadian friends would have gone home had you and Lola not been able to be with us."[10]

Aiken saw a link between positive relations with Canada and his position as a senator from Vermont. Canadian support was crucial not only for the seaway but also for the Champlain Waterway. Although the latter project never received significant support at the highest levels of either government, in 1960 Aiken succeeded in getting the Interparliamentary Group to support referral of the waterway project to the International Joint Commission. He was then able to persuade the commission to conduct a major feasibility study, with extensive hearings on both sides of the border. Its final negative report was one of the major setbacks in his career.[11]

Lynch's remark about Aiken as Quebec's "congressman" is

more apt than even Lynch knew; throughout his senatorial career, Aiken nurtured his contacts with Canada as carefully as he had cared for his Windham County nursery before he entered politics. He had a good nurseryman's patience and farsightedness. He was prepared to plant seedlings, water and tend them, and wait for his plants to flourish. I believe Aiken brought this philosophy to his entire political life, and nowhere is this more evident than in his attitude toward Canada.

A Cartoon by Elderman, 7 December 1937.
© *the* Washington Post.

9

George D. Aiken: A View from the Archives

D. Gregory Sanford

*T*O PREPARE FOR DISCUSSING THE AIKEN LEGACY, I thought I would use the perspectives of students in the Vermont history course I taught at Johnson State College a few years ago. All but one of the students were native Vermonters, and I figured their comments would suggest perceptions of Aiken's legacy. My plans went awry when not a single student had heard of George D. Aiken. In fairness to the students, most of them were two years old when Aiken retired from the Senate in 1975. Still, the students' responses should be startling for anyone examining George Aiken's public career and reflecting on his significance for Vermont and subsequent generations of Vermonters.

My own perspective is personal and professional. It is unusual, perhaps, because my experience with Aiken began when his political career ended. Therefore an assessment of his career awakes intensely personal memories, as well as my historical interest.

Professor Samuel B. Hand once suggested that I was the second largest object to come to the University of Vermont in 1975. The largest was the 750 feet of records documenting the political career of George Aiken. At Sam's urging, I became the first person to spend a substantial amount of time doing research in the Aiken Papers. To be thus associated with George Aiken and the esteem with which he was held opened opportunities not usually accorded a master's candidate. Coupled with the kindness, patience, and interest that Aiken and his wife, Lola, extended to me, these opportunities turned me into a student of the Vermont experience and, eventually, into the Vermont state archivist.

My early research centered on three efforts. The first was to publish an article or two, based on the Aiken Papers, to alert the public to the wealth of information contained in the papers. The result was a collaboration with Sam on Aiken's 1936 gubernatorial campaign, which was published in *Vermont History*.[1] This was the first in a series of collaborations on Aiken and eventually on the Vermont Republican party.

The second effort was to facilitate access to the papers by refining some of the finding aids. Sam and I combed the correspondence from the 1930s. Using rather imprecise criteria, such as the number of times a particular correspondent appeared or our own knowledge of the correspondent's career, we designated a few individuals as significant. We then wrote brief biographical sketches of those correspondents and noted the dates and location of the letters. The final step was to capture Aiken's own memories of the individuals in our index through the use of oral history. We gathered this material and presented it as a supplement to the existing finding aids. After all these years I still think this is an excellent example of how to use oral history as a complement to traditional archival tools.

The third and final effort was my thesis, which was entitled "The Presidential Boomlet for George D. Aiken, 1937–1939, or You Can't Get There from Here."[2] The thesis examined how Governor Aiken skillfully exploited the prestige that Vermont accrued within the Republican party because of its fealty in the 1936 elections. In brief, he used that prestige to publicly challenge the Republican national leadership to offer a positive alternative to the New Deal that would address the needs of the working and middle classes. His challenge enhanced the widespread belief that he would seek the presidential nomination in 1940, a perception Aiken did nothing to discourage. This had the dual effect of further weighting his demands on the party and of augmenting his own battle with Franklin D. Roosevelt over a planned Connecticut River Valley Authority. The latter would have flooded significant portions of Vermont—including Aiken's ancestral home in Dummerston—and curtailed the state's ability to develop its own hydroelectric potential.

Because of these early efforts, I was fortunate enough to be hired as the assistant director of the George D. Aiken Oral History Project, working under the direction of Charles Morrissey. Over the course of five years, from 1975 to 1980, I helped prepare, transcribe, and occasionally conduct oral history interviews with Aiken. The project was sponsored by the University of Vermont as a way to further enrich the resources in the Aiken Papers. One result was the oral history memoir, which the university recently printed as part of the examination of the Aiken legacy.[3]

I have frequently been asked why we would execute such an elaborate oral history project when there were already 750 feet of documents detailing Aiken's career. In part, the answer is quite simple. The Aiken Papers, with the exception of a few early campaign records and some correspondence from the 1930s, document only Aiken's Washington career. By using oral history, we were able to capture Aiken's recollections of his childhood and early manhood and the forces that helped shape his personal and political beliefs.

The interviews also detailed the governor's rise in state politics beginning in 1930. This offered interesting opportunities to combine recorded recollections with traditional documentary sources. To cite one example, Aiken attributed his emergence as a political force to his success in blocking a flood control bill in the Vermont legislature. As Putney's town representative, he opposed the bill because of the extensive control it granted utility companies over the development of the state's energy resources.

The bill had powerful supporters, including the speaker of the Vermont House of Representatives. In the interviews Aiken noted that the House Conservation and Development Committee on which he served was closely split. Always a good vote counter, he could still enumerate, forty-five years later, those committee members who favored the bill. In discussing one of these supporters, Aiken mentioned that she "happened to be absent from the committee at the time we voted to ask the Speaker to withdraw his bill." By checking the committee's minutes at the State Archives, I was able to confirm Aiken's recollection. Indeed, the minutes revealed that several of the bill's supporters were absent that day, suggesting that the timing of the vote was not accidental. Immediately following the vote, the committee selected George Aiken to inform the speaker.

The existence of an extensive documentary record to back up and prod an interviewee's memory is crucial to developing a good oral history. An oral history can, and often should, be done in conjunction with large collections of papers and documents. Even for the years Aiken spent in the U.S. Senate, which are well documented in the papers, the oral histories provide details and bring to light personal relationships that might not be apparent otherwise.

We also conducted oral histories with longtime Aiken associates such as Judge Sterry Waterman and publisher Robert Mitchell. These interviews, though not part of the Aiken project, provide further information about the man and his times.[4]

I confess that over the years I have heard a few complaints about the oral histories. People bemoan the lack of detail about the mechanics of Senate committee work or of getting particular legislation passed. Others have expressed disappointment that there is no greater analysis of Aiken's political colleagues—or, put more bluntly, no juicy tidbits from a senatorial career that spanned World War II, the McCarthy years, Vietnam, and other events that still evoke strong emotions among the public.

As with all oral histories, the answer lies both with the interviewers and the interviewee. From our side of the microphone, I admit we could have done more. In particular, we should have taken better advantage of the Aiken Papers, more consistently using them to jog memories and focus conversations. Had we done so, I suspect that we could have elicited at least some additional information about the mechanics of legislation. But I also believe the nature and personality of George Aiken would never have led him to speculate in detail about the personalities and foibles of his colleagues. He was the consummate politician whose effectiveness stemmed in part from his integrity and loyalty. It simply would have been out of character for him publicly to pick apart or analyze the men and women with whom he had worked for so long.

We have become somewhat jaded today. This is, after all, the age of kiss-and-tell memoirs and of the regular and open dissection of the private lives of public officials and figures. Aiken's reticence about probing the personalities of his colleagues may occasionally frustrate the historian, but it can also be something of a relief, a reminder of a more genteel time.

With the death of George Aiken, the part of his record made up of the oral histories became frozen in time. There is no longer the chance to add a belated insight or to polish a follow-up question. Or perhaps that is not quite true; we could still refine and broaden the materials future researchers will use to understand George Aiken and his times. Surely it is time to conduct systematic and thorough interviews with Lola Aiken. The result would be as full and rich a resource as the interviews with George Aiken.

So far, in my view from the archives, I have focused on the documentary record from which George Aiken's life and career can be examined. As I hope I have suggested, the record is so extensive that it should encourage a deeper analysis of his legacy. But with any body of evidence, there must be public willingness to look anew at the record in order to make fresh discoveries and challenge old nostrums.

Given the opportunities the Aiken Papers present for research, it is interesting to see how over the past sixteen years his records had been used and how we now view that legacy. Having checked use patterns at the State Archives (we hold Aiken's official correspondence) and at the University of Vermont's Special Collections, the index to *Vermont History* for the years 1978–1987, thesis holdings at Special Collections, and other sources to see what had been written, I have learned that use and publication trailed off significantly after the mid-1970s. The Aiken Papers still attract about ten researchers a year. This is a respectable number, though somewhat lower than I would have anticipated. At the State Archives Aiken's official gubernatorial records receive only occasional use; a year or two may pass between requests. The index to *Vermont History* for 1978–1987 reveals only three articles on Aiken, one by me and two by Mark Stoler.[5]

As I noted, my informal survey of Vermont history students revealed that not a single one knew of Governor Aiken. A colleague I asked to conduct a similar survey got the same results. My social acquaintances knew more but only along predictable lines. Their answers were invariably framed by references to the Vietnam War—and more often than not the statement "Declare a victory and get out"—or to how little he spent on campaigns (usually including mention that Aiken's 1968 campaign cost $17.09). Never did I hear reference to Republican progressivism, the St. Lawrence Seaway, Aid to Women with Infants and Children, or any of the myriad other facets of Aiken's career.

So what does all of this mean for the Aiken legacy? I think more than anything else it means that we Vermonters—historians and others—are still trying to figure out what that legacy is. This is a natural process. Historian and bibliographer Kevin Graffagnino suggested to me that Vermonters take at least a generation before they begin to write about their most cherished leaders. Biographies of Ethan Allen, for example, did not appear until almost the mid-nineteenth century, even though the Allens left an extensive written record. Ira had to wait even longer. Senator Justin Smith Morrill, in some ways the Aiken of the nineteenth century, did not receive a full biographical treatment until twenty-six years after he died. A substantive biography of Redfield Proctor was not published until seventy years following his death.

Part of this process of understanding includes an initial phase of mythologizing. Certainly the Allens, particularly Ethan, had to become mythic icons before we could again discuss them as human beings. Morrill went through a similar though not as spectacular period. Early-twentieth-century Republican leaders were constantly measured against the model of Morrill's disinterested statesmanship. At the same time, Morrill's stands on issues, such as his opposition to the Spanish-American War, were never mentioned.

I see this mythologization occurring with George Aiken, particularly in the constant references to his opinion on Vietnam and his campaigning. For now, we seem content to describe him as the quintessential Vermonter or the most important twentieth-century Vermonter and leave it at that.

This is not to say that this process isn't occasionally maddening. For example, with even minor research, someone could clarify and reveal the significance of Aiken's famously frugal campaign spending. Let me be the first to begin. From his race for lieutenant governor in 1934 to his last Senate campaign in 1968, Aiken reported a total of $4,423.03 in campaign expenses. That includes primary and general elections. By way of comparison, in the 1990 U.S. Senate race in Vermont, each candidate spent over $1 million. It is unfortunate that even state representative and senate races are routinely beginning to exceed Aiken's totals.

We mythologize certain figures as a way of understanding and ordering our own lives and society. The degree to which we feel alienated from our present is often expressed in the degree we mythologize and idealize our past.

In a statewide series of programs about state government, presented as part of the Vermont statehood bicentennial in 1991, Vermonters had an opportunity to express their thoughts on contemporary issues. Two common themes emerged. One was that people have come to see government as something entirely distinct from and alien to themselves. This is a sobering thought in a democracy. The second was that something has changed in Vermont. We have become unclear about what being a Vermonter means; we can no longer agree on a common good.

Those perceptions contribute to a renewed interest in George Aiken. They help explain why he is increasingly seen as a symbol of an older, simpler Vermont (and U.S. Senate) where democracy flourished and there was agreement on common goals. His passing has come to mark the loss of innocence, the end of a time when a fruit grower from Putney could achieve state and national leadership—and could achieve it without displaying the nastiness or compromise of values we have all too often come to expect from our leaders.

It is my hope that this nostalgia will eventually lead others to look beyond the symbols and aphorisms to understand both the man George Aiken and the Vermont he represented, to cross the line from mythology to understanding.

Signing the Aiken water bill, October 7, 1965. Left to right: President Lyndon B. Johnson, Governor Philip H. Hoff, Senator Aiken. Courtesy of Bailey/Howe Library, University of Vermont.

10

George D. Aiken: A Personal View from the State House

Philip H. Hoff

*L*ET ME BEGIN WITH SOME DISCLAIMERS. I WAS NOT one of George Aiken's staff members. I am not a historian who has done research on some aspect of George Aiken's life. I was not his intimate friend, although we enjoyed a cordial relationship. And I was not a political ally. In truth, I did not have extensive contact with George Aiken on a person-to-person basis.

I had some very interesting experiences with him, however, and I'll discuss them to illustrate some of his personal qualities— his focus, if you will. And let me suggest that any conference about George Aiken should be one about George and Lola Aiken. They were a team: together they were an effective force for representing Vermont terms and Vermont issues in Washington.

Two critical factors colored my relationship with George Aiken. First, although I never considered running against him,

Aiken had to think of me as a potential challenger. This simple reality, built into the political process, prevented, I think, some of the intimacy that otherwise might have grown up between us, because Aiken and I tended to operate from a common philosophical viewpoint.

Second, my simply having been elected governor signaled a change in the relative strengths of the Republican and Democratic parties in Vermont at that particular time. My election victory in 1962 was the first time the Democrats had won the governorship in over a hundred years. In terms of the popular vote, it was the first time ever, because the last Democratic governor was not elected by the people of Vermont but by the legislature. The Republican party, which had controlled the state for a century, therefore saw me and my colleagues as an emerging problem.

There were two distinct elements within that party: the more conservative wing, generally called the Proctor/industrial wing, and the progressive wing, generally referred to as the Aiken/Gibson wing. It's important to understand that split in terms of the context within which I operated. George Aiken always recognized that much of his support came from the Democratic party.

The Democrats universally backed Aiken, and I can describe that alliance by recalling a story about Ernest Gibson Jr. A fellow by the name of Murphy (a Democrat) who distributed magazines and newspapers throughout the state once told me that when Gibson became a candidate for governor in the 1946 Republican primary against Mortimer Proctor, the Democrats enthusiastically supported him because—and this is almost a quote—he was the closest thing to a Democrat who had a chance of winning that Democrats had seen in the state for a long, long time, and they came out in droves to vote for him in the Republican primary. I don't think that was ever lost on Aiken. He had as many friends within the Democratic party as he had in the Republican party.

So in many ways, but not in the strict political sense, Aiken and I were potential allies, and in that respect we had a cordial relationship. When I went to Washington, I always stopped in to see him. At least once I had the rare privilege of having breakfast with George and Senator Mike Mansfield. That was very unusual, as nobody ever deigned to intrude on that breakfast. I recognize now that it was a great honor. More often, we had lunch together in the Senate dining room.

There was also something of the adviser about him. I knew that if things were tough, I could get a straight answer from Aiken. Two events illustrate this point. I was in Washington when I had pretty much made up my mind that I was going to run for governor a third time. That broke with a long-standing Vermont tradition; it certainly broke with all Republican Vermont traditions. I thought it would be sensible for me to mention it to George and get his reaction. He cautioned that the third term usually brings some troubles; it becomes more difficult because things begin to catch up with you. But he finally encouraged me to go ahead.

I particularly remember another event where I sought Aiken's advice. I had fretted and stewed about the unfortunate war in Southeast Asia. The legislature was just winding down, but I woke up one morning with the conviction that I could not live with the war anymore. So I called an early staff meeting and announced to them that I was going to break with President Lyndon Johnson on the issue. Later I decided it made more sense to support Robert Kennedy in his primary challenge for the presidential nomination, but my initial decision was simply to break with Johnson.

I then called White House staff member Marvin Watson and told him my intention. I wanted the president's staff to know. In return I got more phone calls than you could shake a fist at, including a call from Secretary of State Dean Rusk. Johnson's advisers claimed that there were a lot of things that I didn't understand and some new developments that I should consider. They wanted me to fly down to Washington. I told them that there was no way I could do that because our legislature was just finishing the session and I simply had to be here. Rusk decided to come up with his whole crew. I said, "Well, let me think about that."

And then I called George Aiken. I explained to him what I had done and asked, "Is there anything new out there?" He said, "I admire your courage." That was typical of George; I knew that he had grave reservations about the war. Then he said, "There is nothing new." Now that was not a typical response. If he wanted to, George could give you an ambiguous answer. But if it really counted—and he understood in this case it was very important to me—he gave a straight answer.

Did I have some disappointments in my relationship with Aiken? Yes. When I ran against Winston Prouty for the Senate in 1970, I thought I had an understanding with George. He wouldn't support me, of course, but I thought he wouldn't support Prouty either. I knew some of the pressures that he was under, and I must be frank that this was where George could be vague if he wanted to be. He had by no means promised that he would not support Prouty; I understood that going in. In the end, once he did endorse Prouty, it didn't make any difference. I lost that campaign when I brought a lot of black kids up from Harlem in the Vermont–New York Youth Project. I'd do it again; I think it was the right thing to do. But it cost me the election.

Another disappointing episode in my relations with Aiken I still don't understand. Some of you will recall that we had entered into negotiations with Hydro-Québec to bring in a substantial amount of Canadian power: up to 2 million kilowatts at a rate of just slightly over 4 mills per kilowatt hour. (Compare that to what we are paying now.) This would have gone on for an initial period of twenty years, and we would have built on that; although our original allotment would have come from Churchill Falls, the Canadians intended to use the money for other projects.

We needed enabling legislation in the state to set up a non-profit corporation to import this power. A lot of this was the brainchild of Freddie Fayette,[1] but others worked on the plan. We had every major bonding house in the United States involved as we were talking about millions of dollars. The bill got through the Senate without any problems, but in the House all hell broke loose. In my entire experience I have never seen lobbying like that in the state of Vermont. And much of it was of very doubtful probity. We finally got this bill through the second reading in the house by a rather close vote. The third vote was scheduled to come up after town meeting.

Theodore Riehle,2 who was then in the house, established some sort of contact with Aiken, and Aiken said that he had some reservations about the financing, although he was not specific about what concerned him. Whether his lack of support determined the outcome is hard to say, but we lost that bill. The house voted to put it into a study committee, which effectively killed it. I never quite fathomed Aiken's reservations. The contract we were negotiating would have put Vermont in a perfect position to purchase abundant and inexpensive power for the near future. I probably should have gone to Washington and briefed him, but I did not.

Aiken was the best Vermont politician that I have ever known. In my experience, successful people in almost anything have and are known to have integrity. George Aiken had it up to his ears. It was the prime ingredient, I think, that made him such an effective politician—in the very best sense of the word—in Vermont and in Washington. He was what he was. He never tried to pretend that he was something different. I have often thought of Aiken as essentially a naturalist and a farmer who happened to end up in the U.S. Senate. He was a very humble man. Furthermore, I think he was uneasy with power. He had it and he knew he had it, but he was uncomfortable with it because it could be used inappropriately. I think he was always wary about the potential for abusing power in political life.

My first experience with Aiken was at the Burlington Rotary Club when I was a young lawyer sometime in the 1950s. He came in to talk. I remember being excited about that. He gave a very effective speech, but he did it in what I would call a homespun manner. That was typical of him when he spoke to audiences in Vermont.

There were, it always seemed to me, two George Aikens. The one in Vermont wore red suspenders and spoke in colloquialisms, an old-folks kind of a guy. That homespun quality carried him a long way. He had and cherished certain fundamental Vermont val-

ues: individualism, belief in local government. He identified with
Vermont and Vermonters, and they identified with him. The other
George Aiken was in Washington. That one was modestly dressed
in a suit and was immensely respected by his peers. He did have
power, but he used it judiciously and relied more on respect to
accomplish his political goals.

Let me close by talking about his focus. It would be a serious
mistake to think of George Aiken as a national power. He was not.
Nor did he have any ambitions to be. He was not a reformer. He
was not a shaker and a mover. He had one major focus, and that
was Vermont. If you look at almost every piece of legislation that
he is connected with, you will see that it had a direct impact upon
Vermont or had a Vermont overtone. There was, for example, the
case of Charles Ross, who was a Republican but had been appointed to the Federal Power Commission by President Kennedy. He
must have been filling a partial term because it came up again
when Johnson became president following Kennedy's death.
Johnson showed great reluctance to—in fact clearly stated his
preference against—reappointing Ross to the commission. Ross
was an intimate friend of mine, and I was very interested in his
reappointment. I even went to Washington to see what I could do
to influence that decision. I couldn't spin a thread; the president
wouldn't see me. I talked to the staff people, of course, but I got
nowhere. I came back pretty discouraged. Meanwhile, Aiken was
working on the matter.

One day I got a message from the president's office: "Be in
the White House tomorrow afternoon at 4:00." Nothing more. So
at 4:00 I appeared. They always have difficulty knowing where to
have you wait in the White House depending on who else has an
appointment. They might put you in the room where Eisenhower
used an exercise machine as therapy after his heart attack or in a
room where you can relax. Or they might put you someplace else.
In this case I ended up in the Capital Room. I was sitting there
watching my knuckles when suddenly the door burst open and in
came President Johnson and Senator Everett Dirksen. They were
pounding each other on the chest, sort of he-man stuff; they had

made a deal. And Johnson clearly wanted me to see that they had made a deal. Ross went back on the Federal Power Commission, and William Bagley, a member of the coal lobby, would be added when there was one other person going off. That was the deal. That incident showed the extent and limit of Aiken's influence in Washington: Ross's appointment would not have been made without George Aiken. But I had an impact, too. Johnson later remarked to somebody, "I might have tried to resist George Aiken and I might have resisted Phil Hoff, but the combination was lethal."

Here is another example. In 1963 Addison County suffered a drought. The problem came to my attention as governor, and I went down there. They were digging wells 400 feet and getting just a teacup of water. They were in desperate trouble. So I put in a formal application for help at the Office of Emergency Preparedness. They turned me down. I can remember coming home, seeing the telegram, and feeling a flush go up my face. I fired off a telegram to President Kennedy that said, "They simply do not understand the situation here in Vermont." The next morning Kennedy was on his way to Dallas. The helicopter was in the yard with the rotor slowly turning when Ed McDermott, who was then head of the Office of Emergency Preparedness, received a call from the White House to come over. As McDermott came into the president's office, Kennedy was busy stuffing papers into a briefcase, and he asked, "Ed, what's the story on Vermont?" And Ed said, "Well, I don't really know, but it has something to do with lack of water." "Well, I wish you'd get up there," Kennedy said; "Phil Hoff is a friend of mine." So Kennedy went to Dallas—you know what happened there—and McDermott came up to Vermont. Back in Washington, McDermott found himself in charge of things for a brief period. But we immediately got some help. Then Aiken sponsored the Rural Water Bill to provide rural areas with water. The bill had a Vermont focus. Aiken pulled all his muscle, and it passed. I went down for the signing; I think I had even testified on behalf of the bill. Later Johnson used it as a political tool to come up to Vermont and survey the efforts. I remember that particularly because Aiken and I and several others joined Johnson in the helicopter that flew to Addison County. There was a lot of hoopla, and the president was very pleased.

George Aiken was remarkable by any definition. But I hope we don't deify him. That would be a mistake. He was a human being, and that was part of his greatness, of course. He had a very real sense of all of us as human beings, and it was that ability to relate, I think, that accounted for much of his strength.

Aiken and friends on a fishing trip, June 1938. Left to right: Ralph Flanders, Alf Landon, Aiken, Sterry Waterman. Courtesy of Bailey/Howe Library, University of Vermont.

11

George D. Aiken: A Tribute

James L. Oakes

*A*S WELL AS I KNEW GEORGE AIKEN OVER A PERIOD of time going back almost forty years and despite the many conversations he and I had over the years on matters pertaining to Vermont, I found it was not an easy task to assemble some comments about him that would adequately summarize his accomplishments and his significance for Vermont and U.S. politics. Although so simple on the outside, so down-to-earth, so caring about his state and country, Aiken was an incredibly complex person. His various interests and projects—local, state, national, and international—make it difficult to get at the heart of the man and his work in a brief presentation. In assembling my portrait, I have had the benefit of the revealing oral history memoirs compiled by Charles Morrissey and Gregory Sanford, as well as Aiken's four books: *Pioneering with Wildflowers* (1933), *Pioneering with Fruits and Berries* (1936), *Speaking from Vermont* (1938), and *Aiken: Senate Diary, January 1972–January 1975* (1976).

George Aiken was concerned with his roots. He was proud that they dated back to the 1770s in Vermont, his forebears having come to Windham County apparently by way of New Hampshire, though he did not advertise it. Colonel Edward Aiken was one of the incorporators of Londonderry and a Deacon Edward Aiken was granted the right to develop the town of Windham, Vermont. Another member of his family went south, where, as he put it, "they got a good-sized town named for him": Aiken, South Carolina.

George Aiken's father, Edward, and his mother, Myra Cook Aiken, had a small hill farm in Putney, Vermont. They raised vegetables, berries, and tobacco and had three cows. George Aiken peddled the berries and vegetables in downtown Brattleboro. He didn't like it, he later said, but he had to do it. He milked the cows and helped in the barn with the tobacco, which was grown for cigar wrappers. He always considered himself a hill farmer, and that meant a lot to him because New England hill farmers had a love of liberty; were self-reliant, thrifty, and progressive; and believed in local self-government.

He did not come to politics from out of the blue. "It ran in the family," he said. His father was elected to the Vermont legislature four times and was a supporter of Theodore Roosevelt, whom George Aiken saw speak in Brattleboro when he was a young lad. Edward Aiken and Ernest Gibson Sr. of Brattleboro were fellow Bull Moosers in 1912, and they worked together then as their sons George and Ernest Jr. were later to work together for the greater part of their lives. Aiken considered his father "anti-conservative"—he had it in his blood and it was passed from generation to generation, as the son said—"and he was progressive in a way. He never had any money." Being "progressive" and not having any money may have gone together.

Aiken was educated in Putney, including three years at the high school, where he and two other pupils had the same teacher for all three years. He spent his final year at Brattleboro High School, commuting by train from Putney, nine cents each way. He was the first to admit that he was not a top student at Brattleboro. Geometry, he confessed, gave him considerable trouble. But he was a student of other things: trees, plants, berries, streams, wildflowers. He tells in *Pioneering with Wildflowers* how at age eight, after admiring for some time a clump of dutchman's breeches in the woods, he dug it up one night, brought it home, and planted it under a lilac bush. That transplant thrived for nearly twenty years before the lilac suckers obliterated it. He also speaks of being "philosophical" in his younger days. I am sure he was so and that it stood him in good stead in later years.

George Aiken never went to college. He couldn't afford the $500 it then cost to go to the University of Vermont. Instead, he became active in the Grange, rising to the post of master of the Putney Grange at the ripe old age of eighteen, the year after he graduated from high school. Two years later, with George Darrow, he bought 40 acres of pastureland where he put in a small ice pond and began to raise fruit. Three years out of high school he helped organize the Windham County Farm Bureau, and at the age of twenty-five he was elected president of the Vermont Horticulturist Society. By the time World War I broke out, he had two children, and although he registered for the draft, he was not called to service because he was in the nursery business, raising food. He raised raspberries mostly, and fairly successfully, too. He liked to say later that he had 10,000 customers from all over the state of Vermont but quite a few from out of state as well. Ambassador Sumner Wells, for example, was later to show him some bushes in Washington, D.C., that the Wellses had bought twenty years before from the Aiken Nursery. He told me that Judge Learned Hand, who with his wife had a place in Cornish, New Hampshire, was another regular customer. His nursery was on old Route 5, the main route for travel north and south in Vermont at that time.

Aiken ran for the legislature in 1922 but lost to a Democrat because of a last-minute, false rumor about his being for school centralization. After that defeat he kept his nose pretty much to the grindstone of the nursery business, not running again until 1930, when he was elected. In the meantime he served as a member of the school board through the 1920s and early 1930s. What with nursery customers all over Vermont and his statewide work in the Grange and the Farm Bureau, he had become well known.

He was the first person to raise trailing arbutus commercially, and his raspberry field continued to do well.

When Aiken got back into politics, he thrust himself almost immediately into opposition to the private power companies. The legislature was considering a bill that would effect flood control through cooperation between the state and private utilities. If adopted it would have authorized the power companies to construct dams on virtually every power site in the state and generate hydroelectric power from those dams. Aiken didn't like that at all. The private utilities, he said, would have bought up every dam site on nearly every brook in Vermont where 500 kilowatts of power could be generated. And they would thereby gain "control of the destiny and development of the state." The bill had been introduced by Speaker of the House H. Deavitt. It had the support of the power companies, railroads, granite industry, marble industry, and insurance business in the state. This was George Aiken's first conflict with the "old guard," as he called them.

Aiken was a member of the house Conservation Committee, which had jurisdiction over legislation pertaining to streams and waterpower. He used his knowledge about trees and plants, and some good allies on the committee, to get it to vote against the bill by a majority of one. Deavitt consequently withdrew his bill.

Deavitt was not reelected. Aiken not only was reelected but became speaker of the house in 1932. He thought it was Ernest Gibson Jr. who first suggested he make a bid for speaker. He ran against the "public utility boys." His opponents for speaker were two bankers, and he liked to chuckle at "what chance a banker had of being elected anything in 1933 because all the banks were being closed, being suspected, and so on and so forth."

During that campaign, he went to station WGY in Schenectady to give his first radio talk—on strawberries. He also spoke at the Fair Haven Garden Club and recalled that eighteen of its members brought up *Pioneering with Wildflowers* to be autographed, which suited him fine. Even when he subsequently became a candidate for governor, he tended to speak on anything but politics, usually on trees or plants of some kind. As he said, "I didn't talk politics too much; bring them in incidentally, you know, casual remarks. Sometimes that's more effective, anyway." What lessons he could teach some of today's politicians!

What are some of the recurring themes running through Aiken's political life? First, of course, is Vermont itself. It's why he liked to be called "governor" even after he became a U.S. senator. But he was no xenophobic Vermonter. He welcomed newcomers, second-home buyers, the people who moved to Vermont because they wanted to. He was interested in the development of ski areas in Vermont and indeed as governor signed the first agreement for the ski resort at Mount Mansfield. He foresaw in 1938 that a shorter workweek was bound to come, that distances would be reduced, and that the businessman or the working man of the industrial town who was not within commuting distance would be spending weekends with his family on their own homestead in Vermont. He viewed Vermont as a liberal, progressive, even radical state, a state that very often led the way in experimenting with new programs. He referred to it as "the best" and "the cleanest" state. He was proud that the Vermont constitution was the most radical document of its day, making the state the first to prohibit adult slavery in any form, to extend the right of suffrage to all men regardless of property ownership, and to recognize the subservience of private property to public need, though it required just compensation for taking private land for public use. He saw Vermont, with its natural beauty, as a place where people like to live and "where freedom of thought and action is logical and inherent." He welcomed the professional people, writers, teachers, artists, and others who made their homes in the small villages and on the "abandoned" farms among the hills. He may have come to personify the quintessential Vermonter, but he was already one to start with.

Through his work in the Grange and Farm Bureau and in connection with agriculture, Aiken saw how cooperation can reduce the costs of marketing, secure a fair share of the price the consumer pays, enable standardization of grading and testing, and permit savings in the purchase of farm supplies as well as by sharing risks through insurance and providing capital and credit for agricultural enterprises. He carried this theme from agriculture to other areas, believing in cooperation among labor, management, and government, and opposing it to governmental regulation. This is pretty much the principal thesis of his book *Speaking from Vermont,* a collection of essays and speeches from the 1930s. It was in this book that as governor of Vermont he addressed an open letter to the Republican National Committee in December 1937, and as a result received considerable attention as a possible presidential candidate in 1940. In a chapter entitled "Unless We Cooperate," Aiken preached cooperation as the answer to what he and other Republican critics considered the New Deal's unreasonable regulation and excessive public works programs that paid wages so high that the government competed with private industry for good workers.

He did not, however, see cooperation as a panacea for the country's ills. He was very much concerned with the "humiliation," as he referred to it, of a worker out of work or an employer who couldn't meet his payroll. He recognized that whether times are good or bad, there will always be a number of people who are unemployed, wards of society who cannot work by reason of incapacity of mind or body. He was also interested in having Social Security provide temporary unemployment insurance to cushion the shock, and he was proud that Vermont was one of the first states in the Union to cooperate with every agency of the Social Security Act of 1935 for the relief of human distress. He knew that Social Security was there to stay. The unemployed and unemployable were a lifelong concern of his, as his critical work in connection with food stamps indicated. Time and again when others tried to limit the availability of food stamps, he fought to keep them, as well as school lunches, school milk, and food for infants and mothers. He was proud of Aid to Women, Infants, and Children (WIC, as it is now known), a program he cosponsored with Hubert Humphrey, though he never tooted his own horn about it. He was pleased that the first Head Start program began in East Fairfield, Vermont.

If there was one matter that concerned him throughout his entire life, however, it was agriculture. It was a subject that he knew as well or better than anyone in the country. He was a member of the Agriculture and Forestry Committee from his very first year in the U.S. Senate, 1941, until his retirement in 1975, and he was chairman of the committee from 1953 to 1955. He was ranking member of the Subcommittee on Agricultural Credit and Rural Electrification and during his time in the Senate did more than anyone else to bring rural electrification to this country. He was also a member of the Subcommittee on Environmental Soil Conservation and Forestry and the Subcommittee on Agricultural Appropriations.

He often classified the people he met in the Senate and around the world according to whether or not they were farmers. He got along famously with Senator Charles McNary (R–Ore.), who was an apple farmer. He even remarked favorably on Nikita Khrushchev because he, too, was a farmer. He and two others, trying to help Governor Thomas E. Dewey's 1948 presidential campaign, wrote agricultural position papers for him. Although Dewey had a dairy farm and was a progressive farmer, he declined to use the papers because his advisers wanted him to avoid controversial issues. Aiken recognized that agriculture was "always controversial." He was convinced that Dewey lost the nine states of the Midwest in that election by keeping quiet on agriculture.

Part of Aiken's interest in agriculture was a concern for conservation, though he was not a radical environmentalist. He believed in balance. As a fruit farmer he had sprayed against bud moths and applied powdered arsenate of lead to the soil before planting strawberries. Nevertheless, he guided the first pesticide bill through the Senate in 1947 and twenty-five years later secured passage of the Federal Environmental Pesticide Control Act.

As I have already mentioned, it was the "public utility boys" who started him off in politics, and he continued to oppose them throughout his career. He and Ernest Gibson Jr. often fought side by side to protect Vermont's Connecticut River hydropower sources from being taken over by utilities bent upon harnessing them to provide power to southern New England. They also worked hard to promote the St. Lawrence Seaway legislation that enabled Vermont to have the lowest power costs in New England from 1960 to 1990. In the 1930s Samuel Insull and his businesses milked Vermont electricity companies, specifically the Green Mountain Power Company, and their customers for the benefit of public utility holding company investors. As governor, Aiken called in both the Federal Securities and Exchange Commission and the Federal Power Commission to look into Insull's activities.

From Washington, D.C., Aiken continued to watch over Vermont's interests in power issues. I had several talks with Senator Aiken in the days when Charles Ross was chairman of the Vermont Public Service Board under Governor Robert Stafford, and we were dealing with the utility companies on behalf of the state as well as attempting to negotiate for Niagara Power. Aiken recognized Ross's enormous talent and willingness to fight. He was instrumental in getting President John F. Kennedy to appoint Ross to the Federal Power Commission in 1960 and then in getting President Lyndon Johnson to retain him on the International Joint Commission overseeing the boundary waters of Canada and the United States. As federal power commissioner, Ross wrote a dissent in what became the famous Scenic Hudson case, which served as the springboard for the national Environmental Policy Act of 1969. Although Aiken was himself a conservationist and struggled from time to time with the power companies, he was a believer in the efficacy of nuclear power, and he and his wife, Lola, were good friends of Admiral Hyman Rickover, called the father of the U.S. nuclear navy. Lola even christened a nuclear submarine.

Three other themes within Aiken's life warrant at least brief mention. First was his interest in youth, particularly young Republicans; he came to know and like, among others, Sterry Waterman, Leon Latham, Winston Prouty, Peter Bove, and Luke Crispe.[1] Those friendships ran deep, and it was the appointment of Waterman to the U.S. Court of Appeals, Second Circuit, over the objection of some people in New York, that preserved Vermont's seat on the court where I sat, and where Waterman served his state and country so well.

Second is Aiken's interest in international affairs and foreign relations. He was extremely concerned about U.S. relations with Mexico and Canada, and in his capacity as a member of the Senate Foreign Relations Committee for twenty-one years he often worked with his counterparts in Canadian government. He was also interested in Far Eastern affairs, Western Hemisphere affairs, the nuclear test ban treaty of 1963, the United Nations, and U.S. relations with the Soviet Union. He was a cosponsor of Food for Peace, one of the major instruments of U.S. foreign policy. I can attest that he was influential in but is rarely credited with the change in this country's policy toward Rhodesia during the internal struggle for home rule by the African majority. His support for a prohibition on importing Rhodesian chromium helped turn the tide toward the establishment of at least some form of democracy in that colonial African country. He and I talked much about it after I made a visit to Zambia for the State Department Agency for International Development in 1971.

Third, Aiken's approach to political parties is worth noting: even though he generally supported the Republican party and the party's presidents, he was too independent simply to listen to the old guard. During his years in the U.S. Senate, his work for the state of Vermont was helped more, perhaps, over breakfast with Senator Mike Mansfield of Montana or a talk with Senator James Eastland than it was by party politics.

Finally, Aiken's integrity is legendary. He was never tempted by the little things—free hotel rooms, gifts, airplane rides—that beguile so many of our so-called public servants. He told of other members of Congress who went to private hunting preserves or stayed at a hotel in White Sulphur Springs or used New England industrialist Bernard Goldfine's [2] hotel suite in Boston or the like. Offered a suite at the Hotel Roosevelt in New York (which had a Vermont manager), he paid for the room and said, "If you want to throw in the suite I don't care because I am not going to use but one room." Commenting on that episode, he later added, "I don't think they were trying to work me for anything except I was from Vermont and they had great friends in Vermont. But that's the way they do." He would not accept gifts over fifty dollars, whether it came from a single friend or an entire country. And of course his famous campaign of 1968, on which he spent $17.09, comes to mind. So does Lola's going off the payroll the day she and Aiken were married, June 30, 1967, even though she continued her full-time job as Aiken's office manager for seven and a half more years. Even his retirement cost him: had he resigned before midnight on December 31, 1974, he could have added 7.4 percent to his retirement pay, but he did not choose to do so "because I have always felt I should carry out contracts in full." After having been elected to the Senate in 1940, he insisted on completing his term as governor of Vermont, losing a week's pay as senator; he was never sorry he did that.

Aiken always did what he thought was right for the country and right for the state, never by calculating the personal good or harm that would come to friend or foe or the status of people with whom he had to deal. He was extremely modest. He admired Senator Robert Taft (R–Ohio), who would go to someone's office to talk instead of asking the person to come over and see him. This was the way Aiken was, too. He treated everybody, big or small, with the same respect; he made the people who worked *for* him feel as though they worked *with* him.

He was also flexible. Time and again he said that if you can't get 100 percent of what you want, settle for 90 or 80 or 70 percent, but if it gets down to around 60, maybe you had better think it over. A perfect example was the Bricker amendment, which would have drastically curtailed the president's powers in respect to treaties. Having signed on as one of about seventy-two sponsors, he voted against the bill once the American Bar Association split on it. It died in the Senate by one vote.

Although many sources, including *Time* magazine, gave Senator Everett Dirksen of Illinois the credit for working the compromise that passed the Civil Rights Act of 1964, Aiken was on the bipartisan committee of seven senators (Aiken, Dirksen,

Hubert Humphrey, Thomas Kuchel, Warren Magnuson, Mike Mansfield, and Leverett Saltonstall) who cooperated with the office of Attorney General Robert Kennedy to enable passage of the bill. I have always thought—and I happened to be present on the Hill during the Senate vote on the bill—that it was George Aiken who conceived of the compromise that led to the bill's passage. The compromise was designed to protect the little person, exempting from fair housing regulation "Mrs. Murphy," the fictitious woman who rented out only a few rooms. Aiken at least told the president that "we want you to let Mrs. Murphy alone," and I distinctly remember his mentioning Mrs. Murphy to me the day before the vote.

Aiken was a wise old owl. That is how I knew him. He was not a politician in the negative sense of the word, because he always voted for what he thought was right or against what he thought was wrong. But he was a consummate politician in the positive sense of the word, and not just because he could compromise—up to a point. In speaking he would go on a tangent. Lola has suggested that he would sometimes answer a different question from the one he was asked because he "didn't want" to respond to the initial question. One newspaper reporter thought that he was fuzzy or uncertain in his latter days in the Senate. This wasn't at all true. As he put it, "Sometimes a speaker can fend off a more difficult situation by diverging from the subject." Like Abraham Lincoln, he would never lie but would shift the argument to his own advantage and thereby get himself off the hook. In a sense, this is how I think he may have arrived at his solution for ending the Vietnam War. Half the people wanted us out of the war altogether, and the other half, give or take some percentage points, wanted us to win the war. His solution was to say we won and get out and save lives and resources.

I know he was a good friend of Margaret Chase Smith, and he had been on the President's Commission on the Status of Women. He went to the Republican National Convention of 1964, only his second, to nominate her for president. My family and I were at that convention also, because I was active in the

Rockefeller campaign. (Indeed, my daughter Cynthia and Lola were roommates at the hotel in San Francisco—poor Lola, with a teenager's clothes all over the floor.) That was the year of the battle between Nelson Rockefeller and Barry Goldwater; Goldwater won by carrying California by a whisker, but the Republican party split into two massive segments in Vermont as throughout the country. It was a pretty wise decision on Aiken's part to be for Margaret Chase Smith in those circumstances. I only wish that I could have learned more of those lessons from him in the days when I was in politics and before he made it possible for me to be first a district judge (succeeding his lifelong friend Ernest Gibson) and then judge on the Second Circuit Court of Appeals.

I end on three small, personal grace notes, so to speak, three things for which I especially treasure George Aiken. One of them is a speech in Burlington, Vermont, at a dinner given in his honor in the late winter or early spring of 1971, after he had proposed me as circuit judge with seemingly no result from the administration. He alluded to an instance I had not known about and he had never before mentioned: one day back in about 1950 Judge Learned Hand had told Senator Aiken to keep an eye on me. I had been a young law clerk on what became my court, working for Judge Harrie B. Chase of Brattleboro; this was a link to the great Learned Hand that I never knew I had. The second thing is a little inscription Aiken wrote in his book *Aiken: Senate Diary*: he began, "To Jim, a credit to his state" and ended with words I will always treasure, "also a friend of mine."

Finally, there is the cane. When Aiken and Lola built the little house on Putney Mountain where they could look east to Monadnock, it was his return to a hill farm. Carved out on a rather steep hillside, the berry farm and vegetable garden were constantly prey to the local wildlife. Aiken would work on that hillside without a cane. One day he and I were picking berries, and he slipped. I managed to catch him, needing only one hand to prevent his fall because he then weighed so little. Lola said to us privately that maybe now he would get and use a cane. So my wife, Deede, and I kept our eyes out for just the right one. We knew he wouldn't want any store-bought, fancy affair. At an auction in Westminster a few days later, Deede spent four or five dollars on a cane made locally out of gnarled apple wood. It was perfect. We rushed right down to give it to him. At first he was delighted with it, and then he quickly asked how much it cost—he still wouldn't accept expensive gifts. When we told him the price, he said, "That's all right." He kept the cane until his dying day, and it is with him now.

Notes

Introduction

1. George D. Aiken, *Speaking from Vermont* (New York: Frederick A. Stokes, 1938), 1.

2. George D. Aiken, speech to the 1936 Republican convention, crate 82, box 2, folder 3, Aiken Papers, Special Collections, Bailey/-Howe Library, University of Vermont.

3. Ibid.

4. Aiken, *Speaking from Vermont*, 3, 5.

5. Ibid., 17; see also 13.

6. *Congressional Record*, 85th Cong., 1st sess., 1957, vol. 103, pt. 9, 11872.

Chapter 1

1. "George D. Aiken Oral History Memoir," interviews by Charles T. Morrissey and D. Gregory Sanford, 1981, Folklore and Oral History Archives, Bailey/Howe Library, University of Vermont, 21–22.

2. George D. Aiken, *Aiken: Senate Diary, January 1972–January 1975* (Brattleboro, Vt.: Stephen Greene Press, 1976).

3. Winston Churchill, *Coniston* (New York: Macmillan, 1906).

4. Winston Churchill, *Mr. Crewe's Career* (New York: Macmillan, 1906).

5. Reprinted in Arthur M. Schlesinger Jr., *History of U.S. Political Parties*, vol. 2 (New York: Chelsea House, 1973), 1033.

6. Ibid., vol. 3, 2583.

7. The summary of New Hampshire progressivism follows James Wright, *The Progressive Yankees: Republican Reformers in New Hampshire, 1906–1916* (Hanover: University Press of New England, 1987).

8. Reprinted in William Jewett Tucker, *Public Mindedness: An Aspect of Citizenship Considered in Various Addresses Given While President of Dartmouth College* (Concord: Rumford Press, 1910), 188.

9. For Churchill, see Robert W. Schneider, *Five Novelists of the Progressive Era* (New York: Columbia University Press, 1965), chapter 5; Warren Titus, *Winston Churchill* (New York: Twayne, 1963), especially chapter 3; also Wright, *The Progressive Yankees*, 54–56.

10. 22 October 1910.

11. The most substantial study of Vermont progressivism remains Winston Allen Flint, *The Progressive Movement in Vermont* (Washington, D.C.: American Council on Foreign Affairs, 1941).

12. A letter to Theodore Roosevelt Jr., quoted by Charles Morrissey in Morrissey and Sanford, "Aiken Oral History," 32.

13. Ibid.

14. An overview of Vermont republicanism is William Doyle, *The Vermont Political Tradition: And Those Who Helped Make It* (Montpelier: Privately printed, 1984), especially chapters 7–9.

15. "Open Letter to the Republican National Committee from George D. Aiken, Governor of the State of Vermont," in George D. Aiken, *Speaking from Vermont* (New York: Frederick A. Stokes, 1938), 223. See also Samuel B. Hand and D. Gregory Sanford, "Carrying Water on Both Shoulders: George D. Aiken's 1936 Gubernatorial Campaign in Vermont," *Vermont History* 43, 4 (1975): 292–306.

16. Charles William Tobey (1880–1953) served in the New Hampshire House of Representatives at various times between 1915 and 1926 and was governor of New Hampshire from 1929 to 1930. He was elected to the U.S. House of Representatives for three terms March 1933 to January 1939 and to the U.S. Senate in 1938, 1944, and 1950.

17. David M. Oshinsky, *A Conspiracy So Immense: The World of Joe McCarthy* (New York: Free Press, 1983), 164.

18. Morrissey and Sanford, "Aiken Oral History," 127.

19. Aiken, *Speaking from Vermont*, 5.

Chapter 2

1. John Herbers, "Occupation: Farmer, Avocation: Senator," *New York Times Magazine,* 29 January 1967, 30.

2. "George D. Aiken Oral History Memoir," interviews by Charles T. Morrissey and D. Gregory Sanford, 1981, Folklore and Oral History Archives, Bailey/Howe Library, University of Vermont, 45.

3. *White River Valley Herald,* 20 April 1961.

4. *Rutland Herald,* 4 May 1965.

5. *New York Times,* 20 November 1954.

6. *Brattleboro Daily Reformer,* 10 November 1954.

7. David W. Reinhard, *The Republican Right Since 1945* (Lexington: University Press of Kentucky, 1983), 147–148.

8. *Burlington Free Press,* 8 April 1961.

9. Nicol C. Rae, *The Decline and Fall of the Liberal Republicans: From 1952 to the Present* (New York: Oxford University Press, 1989), 81.

10. Ibid., 85.

11. Ibid., 86.

12. *Rutland Herald,* 4 May 1965.

13. Aiken to Barry Goldwater, 4 January 1964, crate 11, box 2, Aiken Papers, Special Collections, Bailey/Howe Library, University of Vermont.

14. Aiken to Mrs. Ramon Lawrence, 4 August 1966, crate 11, box 2, Aiken Papers.

15. Rae, *Liberal Republicans,* 88.

16. Aiken to Edward W. Porter, 22 July 1968, crate 11, box 2, Aiken Papers.

17. *Washington Post,* 13 January 1960.

18. Aiken to Rita Finnell, 6 February 1971, crate 51, box 4, Aiken Papers.

19. Claudia Townsend, *Ralph Nader Congress Project: George D. Aiken* (Washington, D.C.: Grossman, 1972), 2.

20. Ibid.

21. Ibid.

22. George D. Aiken, "Reminiscences of the Senate," *Boston Sunday Globe,* 13 June 1976, 9.

23. Aiken to Mr. and Mrs. Kenneth Webb, 8 May 1972, crate 51, box 4, Aiken Papers.

24. George D. Aiken, *Aiken: Senate Diary, January 1972–January*

1975 (Brattleboro, Vt.: Stephen Greene Press, 1976), 174, 191.

25. Godfrey Sperling Jr. to Aiken, 25 July 1973, crate 51, box 4, Aiken Papers.

26. *Brattleboro Reformer,* 24 October 1973.

27. Aiken, *Senate Diary,* 239.

28. Ibid., 316.

29. Market Opinion Research 1974, crate 11, box 7, Aiken Papers.

30. Stephen Hess and David S. Broder, *The Republican Establishment* (New York: Harper and Row, 1967), 276.

31. Michael Barone, Grant Ujifusa, and Douglas Matthews, *The Almanac of American Politics, 1976* (New York: Dutton, 1975), 865.

32. Rae, *Liberal Republicans,* 79–80.

33. *National Journal,* 21 October 1991, 2522.

Chapter 3

1. George D. Aiken, *Aiken: Senate Diary, January 1972–January 1975* (Brattleboro, Vt.: Stephen Greene Press, 1976), 259, 268–269.

2. Norman J. Ornstein et al., *Vital Statistics on Congress, 1987–1988* (Washington, D.C.: Congressional Quarterly, 1987), 142–146.

3. Robert C. Byrd, *The Senate, 1789–1989: Addresses on the History of the United States Senate,* vol. 1 (Washington, D.C.: U.S. Government Printing Office, 1989), 537–550.

4. Francis O. Wilcox, Oral History Interviews, Senate Historical Office, 34–35.

5. Pat M. Holt, Oral History Interviews, Senate Historical Office, 278.

6. Ibid., 46.

7. Aiken, *Senate Diary,* 13–14, 155.

8. Ibid., 158; Carl M. Marcy, Oral History Interviews, Senate Historical Office, 191.

9. *Congressional Record,* 93d Cong., 2d sess., 1974, S21025–S21027.

10. Milton R. Young Oral History, University of North Dakota, tape 7, 6.

11. "George D. Aiken Oral History Memoir," interviews by Charles T. Morrissey and D. Gregory Sanford, 1981, Folklore and Oral History Archives, Bailey/Howe Library, University of Vermont, 137.

12. Ibid., 96–97.

13. Floyd M. Riddick, Oral History Interviews, Senate Historical Office.

14. Aiken, *Senate Diary,* 133-134, 144, 159; Morrissey and Sanford, "Aiken Oral History," 91.

15. Norris Cotton, *In the Senate: Amidst the Conflict and Turmoil* (New York: Dodd, Mead, 1978).

16. Aiken, *Senate Diary,* 8–9.

17. Ibid., 12–13, 24–25, 176.

18. See Donald A. Ritchie, *Press Gallery: Congress and the Washington Correspondents* (Cambridge: Harvard University Press, 1991).

19. Morrissey and Sanford, "Aiken Oral History," 136–137.

20. Aiken, *Senate Diary,* 274.

21. *Washington Star,* 10 January 1970; Ornstein et al., *Vital Statistics on Congress,* 77.

22. *Burlington Free Press,* 20 November 1984.

23. Aiken, *Senate Diary,* 342, 345; Morrissey and Sanford, "Aiken Oral History," 90.

24. *Burlington Free Press,* 20 November 1984.

Chapter 5

1. Mary Beth Norton et al., *A People and a Nation,* 3d ed. (Boston: Houghton Mifflin, 1990), A-18, A-21.

2. David Brinkley, *Washington Goes to War* (New York: Knopf, 1988), 75–76.

3. Norton, *A People and a Nation,* A-21.

4. "George D. Aiken Oral History Memoir," interviews by Charles T. Morrissey and D. Gregory Sanford, 1981, Folklore and Oral History Archives, Bailey/Howe Library, University of Vermont, 34.

5. Ibid., "Aiken Oral History," 24.

6. George D. Aiken, *Aiken: Senate Diary, January 1972–January 1975* (Brattleboro, Vt.: Stephen Greene Press, 1976), 150, 184.

7. "Reorganization of Federal Business Enterprises," *U.S. Commission on Organization of the Executive Branch of Government* (also known as the Hoover Commission Reports) (1949), vol. 1, section 6, 114–116.

8. Senate Committee on Foreign Relations, hearing, *St. Lawrence Seaway and Power Project,* 82d Cong., 2d sess., 26 February 1952, 89–90.

9. Morrissey and Sanford, "Aiken Oral History," 115.

10. Among his Senate speeches on the subject, see the Congressional Record, 23 February 1948, 1526–1529.

11. Senate Committee on Agriculture and Forestry, *Policies and Operation Under Public Law 480,* 85th Cong., 1st sess., 1957, 443–444; Aiken, *Senate Diary,* 80.

12. See, for example, Aiken's speeches in the *Congressional Record,* 19 February 1947, 1164–1165; and 24 February 1956, 3317–3319.

13. Senate Committee on Agriculture and Forestry, hearing, *Policies and Operations Under Public Law 480,* 85th Cong., 1st sess., 1957, 486. Also Morrissey and Sanford, "Aiken Oral History," 103.

14. U.S. Congress, *Policies and Operations Under Public Law 480,* 73.

15. Aiken himself was not above pointing out that butter had not been moving fast enough. Senate Committee on Agriculture and Forestry, hearing, *1955 General Farm Situation and Exporting of Surplus Commodities,* 84th Cong., 1st sess., 30.

16. Many passages in Aiken's *Diary* describe the dinners, meetings with foreign leaders, and invitations to the White House. See, for example, 267, 271–272, 290.

17. Aiken, *Senate Diary,* 120.

Chapter 6

1. Gaddis Smith, *Dean Acheson* (New York: Cooper Square, 1972), 416.

2. Lester Markel, "Opinion—A Neglected Instrument," in Lester Markel, ed., *Public Opinion and Foreign Policy* (New York: Harper and Brothers, 1949), 4.

3. This data and several of the points made here are more fully developed in Thomas G. Paterson, *On Every Front: The Making and Unmaking of the Cold War,* 2d ed. (New York: W. W. Norton, 1992).

4. Truman quoted in U.S. Department of State, *Peace, Freedom, and World Trade* (Washington, D.C.: U.S. Department of State, 1947), 5; *Economist,* 24 May 1947, 785.

5. J. William Fulbright, *The Arrogance of Power* (New York: Random House, 1966).

6. Jack Ohman cartoon, quoted in Thomas G. Paterson, *Meeting*

the Communist Threat: Truman to Reagan (New York: Oxford University Press, 1988), 235.

7. "George D. Aiken Oral History Memoir," interviews by Charles T. Morrissey and D. Gregory Sanford, 1981, Folklore and Oral History Archives, Bailey/Howe Library, University of Vermont, 157.

8. Quoted in Paterson, *Meeting,* 169.

9. Quoted in George C. Herring, *America's Longest War: The United States and Vietnam, 1950–1975,* 2d ed. (New York: Knopf, 1986), 155.

10. Robert L. Heilbroner, "Making a Rational Foreign Policy Now," *Harper's,* September 1968, 65.

11. Quoted in Michael Maclear, *The Ten Thousand Day War* (New York: St. Martin's, 1981), 57.

12. Quoted in Walter Goldstein, "The Erosion of the Superpowers: The Military Consequences of Economic Distress," *SAIS Review* 8 (Summer/Fall 1988), 57.

13. Thomas G. Paterson, *On Every Front: The Making and Unmaking of the Cold War* (New York: W. W. Norton, 1992), 183.

14. Goldstein, "Erosion of the Superpowers," 54.

15. George D. Aiken, *Aiken: Senate Diary, January 1972–January 1975* (Brattleboro, Vt.: Stephen Greene Press, 1976), 8, 105, 108, 156, 215.

16. *Public Papers of the Presidents of the United States: Ronald Reagan, 1983,* vol. 1 (Washington, D.C.: U.S. Government Printing Office, 1984), 256.

17. *Weekly Compilation of Presidential Documents* 26 (17 September 1990), 1359, 1360.

18. Message of 29 January 1991, *Congressional Record,* 102d Cong., 1st sess., 1991, 137, pt. 19:1216.

19. *New York Times,* 10 February 1991.

20. Thomas McCormick, *America's Half-Century: U.S. Foreign Policy in the Cold War* (Baltimore: Johns Hopkins University Press, 1989), 216.

21. Marshall D. Shulman, "The Superpowers: Dance of the Dinosaurs," *Foreign Affairs: America and the World, 1987/1988* 66, 3 (1988): 494.

Chapter 7

1. D. Gregory Sanford, "You Can't Get There from Here: The Presidential Boomlet for Governor George D. Aiken, 1937–1939,"

Vermont History 49, 4 (1981): 197–208.

2. *Congressional Record,* 77th Cong., 1st sess., 1941, 87, pt. 2:360–363.

3. Ibid., 79th Cong., 1st sess., 1945, 91, pt. 3:3471–3472; 80th Cong., 1st sess., 1947, 93, pt. 10:1164–1167; Stephen D. Brown, "Senator George D. Aiken and the Place of American Agriculture in the World, 1941–1957," M.A. thesis, University of Vermont, 1970; Dan Cordtz, "Vermont's Aiken," *Wall Street Journal,* 3 March 1966, 14.

4. Some commentators claimed that as a liberal Republican supporter of the postwar bipartisan foreign policy, Aiken also requested the Foreign Relations seat to prevent it from going to the red-baiting Joseph McCarthy. Aiken later denied any such motivation, but his beliefs indicate he definitely preferred the bipartisan Foreign Relations to the intensely partisan Labor Committee. See John Herbers, "Occupation: Farmer, Avocation: Senator," *New York Times Magazine,* 29 January 1967; Aiken to Stephen Brown, 21 November 1967, crate 80, box 4, GDA Views 1962–1969 folder, Aiken Papers, Special Collections, Bailey/Howe Library, University of Vermont.

5. See *Congressional Record* speeches cited in note 3 as well as in 80th Cong., 1st sess., 1947, 93, pt. 11:2787–2788, and 85th Cong., 1st sess., 1957, 103, pt. 4:4872–4873.

6. Ibid., 77th Cong., 1st sess., 1941, 87, pt. 2:360–363.

7. See Duane Tannenbaum, *The Bricker Amendment Controversy: A Test of Eisenhower's Political Leadership* (Ithaca: Cornell University Press, 1988), 70.

8. *Congressional Record,* 85th Cong., 2d sess., 1958, 104, pt. 13:16657; 86th Cong., 2d sess., 1960, 106, pt. 10:13351; 87th Cong., 1st sess., 1961, 107, pt. 3:3170.

9. Aiken speech before World Affairs Council, Boston, 20 May 1960, reprinted in *Congressional Record,* 86th Cong., 2d sess., 1960, 106, pt. 8:10775–10777. See also speeches in ibid., pts. 2–3:1878 and 3434; and 85th Cong., 2d sess., 1958, 104, pts. 8–9:10396 and 12152.

10. May 1961 handwritten evaluation of Aiken, Aiken folder, box 17, Lawrence O'Brien Papers, White House Staff Files, John F. Kennedy Papers, John F. Kennedy Library, Boston. A Kennedy administration assessment of Aiken's voting record is also in the White House Staff Files, Desuatels, box 1.

11. See *Congressional Record,* 82d Cong., 1st sess., 1951, 97, pts. 1

and 2:166 and 2320–2323; 2d sess., 1952, 98, pt. 1:871. See also Aiken to Arthur D. Austin, 3 August 1950, and to Laurence H. Willis, 29 August 1950, crate 6, box 1A, War Legislation 1950 folder, Aiken Papers; Aiken to Dr. Walter G. Weatherhead, 11 December 1950, to Richard M. Judd, 15 December 1950, to Borden E. Avery, 10 January 1951, to Mrs. Richard Sullivan, 4 April 1951, and to Mrs. Arthur H. Hobson, 24 November 1951, crate 39, box 1, Foreign Affairs 1950–1952 folder, Aiken Papers.

12. *Congressional Record*, 89th Cong., 1st sess., 1965, 111, pt. 11: 15320; 2d sess., 1966, 112, pt. 2:1577.

13. Indeed, Aiken stated on numerous occasions that he knew little about Asia and relied on Mansfield for advice in this area, and numerous reporters concluded that Aiken was simply verbalizing Mansfield's thoughts. Mansfield, however, insisted that Aiken was not acting as his mouthpiece and that he had learned at least as much from the Vermonter as Aiken had learned from him. Furthermore, their views on Vietnam were never exactly the same, and by 1968 the divergence had become quite sharp. See Aiken comments on "Issues and Answers" television program, 7 May 1961, reprinted in *Congressional Record,* 87th Cong., 1st sess., 1961, 107, pt. 6:7587–7590; 89th Cong., 1st sess., 1965, 111, pt. 17:23057; Herbers, "Occupation: Farmer"; Drew Pearson column in *Washington Post*, 6 August 1965; and Senate Foreign Relations Committee, hearings, *International Development and Security*, 87th Cong., 1st sess., 1961, 670.

14. *Congressional Record*, 89th Cong., 2d sess., 1966, pt. 2:1576–1577.

15. *Burlington Free Press*, 27 April 1967. See also *Bennington Banner*, 2 August 1967, and *Congressional Record*, 90th Cong., 1st sess., 1967, 113, pts. 4, 10, and 15:4870–4871, 12582, and 19830.

16. A good summation of Aiken's views of executive power can be found in his reply to graduate student Peter R. Chaveas, 16 January 1968, crate 51, box 4, GDA Views 1962–1969 folder, Aiken Papers. See also his letters to Ronald Bonneau, 11 January 1962, and to David Montagu, 13 February 1962, crate 39, box 1; Foreign Relations folder, and to Rev. and Mrs. John H. Lever, 5 March 1964, and to John Parke, 13 March 1964, crate 39, box 2, Asia 1964 folder.

17. Quotes from Aiken to Mrs. Carl Anderson, 12 September 1963, crate 39, box 2, Foreign Aid 1963 folder, Aiken Papers, and

Senate Foreign Relations Committee, hearings, *Review of Foreign Policy,* 1958, 85th Cong., 2d sess., 1958, pt. 1:249. See also transcript of Aiken oral history tape on Eisenhower administration, 1967, crate 65, box 1, Aiken Papers; Aiken to Jeannette A. Smith, 20 May 1954, and to Mrs. Paul Blanchard, 11 June 1954, crate 39, box 1, Foreign Relations Committee 1950s folder, Aiken Papers; Senate Foreign Relations Committee, hearings, *United States Foreign Policy,* 87th Cong., 1st sess., 1961, 255–256.

18. Transcript of Aiken oral history tape on Johnson administration, 10 October 1968, crate 65, box 1, Aiken Papers; George D. Aiken, *Aiken: Senate Diary, January 1972–January 1975* (Brattleboro, Vt.: Stephen Greene Press, 1976), 134–135; *Congressional Record,* 91st Cong., 2d sess., 1970, 116, pt. 29: 38593–38594.

19. Second Bundy draft of "Memorandum for Discussion, Alternative Public Positions for U.S. on Southeast Asia for the Period July 1–November 15," 12 June 1964, National Security File, National Security Council History, container 39, tab 25, Lyndon B. Johnson Papers, Lyndon Baines Johnson Library, Austin, Texas. For information on the Tonkin Gulf crisis, see George C. Herring, *America's Longest War: The United States and Vietnam, 1950–1975,* 2d ed. (New York: Knopf, 1986), 119–123.

20. Lyndon B. Johnson, *The Vantage Point: Perspectives of the Presidency, 1963–1969* (New York: Holt, Rinehart, and Winston, 1971), 116–117.

21. See Mark A. Stoler, "Aiken, Mansfield, and the Tonkin Gulf Crisis: Notes from the Congressional Leadership Meeting at the White House, August 4, 1964," *Vermont History* 50, 2 (1982), 80–94.

22. *Congressional Record,* 88th Cong., 2d sess., 1964, 110, pt. 14:18456–18457.

23. If the administration felt that such legislative action was no longer necessary, he sarcastically wrote to Secretary of State Dean Rusk in early 1965, then he would be most interested in seeing its proposed constitutional amendment. *Congressional Record,* 88th Cong., 2d sess., 1964, 110, pt. 14:18456–18457; 89th Cong., 1st sess., 1965, 111, pts. 5–7:5925–5930, 8125, 9499; 89th Cong., 2d sess., 1966, 112, pt. 2:1576–1577; Aiken to Dean Rusk, 19 May 1965, crate 39, box 27, Southeast Asia Important Material 1965 folder, Aiken Papers.

24. Quotes from *Congressional Record,* 89th Cong., 1st sess., 1965,

111, pt. 5:5925–5927, and *Burlington Free Press*, 21 February 1966. See also Aiken speech at conference on Vietnam and Southeast Asia, Montpelier, Vermont, 23 April 1966, crate 39, box 4, Foreign Relations General 1966 folder 1, Aiken Papers.

25. See *Congressional Record*, 89th Cong., 1st sess., 1965, 111, pt. 11:15320, and 2d sess., 1966, 112, pt. 2:1577. Mansfield's letters and Johnson's replies are in the National Security File, container 6, Johnson Papers.

26. Senate Foreign Relations Committee, Report of Senators Mansfield, Muskie, Inouye, Aiken, and Boggs, *The Vietnam Conflict: The Substance and the Shadow*, 6 January 1966. See also memo, Mansfield to President Johnson, 18 December 1965, "Summary of Conclusions of the Report on Viet Nam," National Security File, container 32, International Meetings and Travel File, Senator Mansfield's Trip folder, Johnson Papers.

27. Johnson ordered his staff to prepare detailed replies to Mansfield's letters. See National Security File, container 6, Johnson Papers.

28. Senate Foreign Relations Committee, hearings, *Foreign Assistance Act: Supplemental, Vietnam*, 89th Cong., 2d sess., 1966, pt. 1:38–40, 514–515, 503–597. The public response to the hearings was both overwhelming and surprising. Although Aiken quipped that television exposure guaranteed the committee a quorum at its sessions, he was truly amazed by the volume and quality of mail that now began to pour into his office. The hearings, he concluded, had made the American people do "more thinking" about Vietnam and China "than I have ever known before." Quotes from Aiken to Murray Hoyt, 19 May 1966, crate 39, box 28, Southeast Asia Vermont Correspondence folder 3, Aiken Papers. See also Aiken's letter to Ralph Nading Hill in folder 1; transcript of Aiken oral history tape on Johnson in crate 55, box 4; and Maurice J. Goldbloom, "The Fulbright Revolt," *Commentary*, 5 September 1966, 63–69.

29. *Congressional Record*, 89th Cong., 2d sess., 1966, 112, pt. 2:1576–1577.

30. Ibid., pt. 20:27525.

31. Transcript of Aiken oral history tape on Johnson administration, 10 October 1968, crate 65, box 1, Aiken Papers.

32. *Congressional Record*, 89th Cong., 2d sess., 1966, 112, pt. 20:27523–27525.

33. *Burlington Free Press* editorial, 20 October 1968.

34. Ibid.; press clippings on GDA Vietnam speech, crate 39, box

5, 19 October 1966 folder, Aiken Papers. See also Mark A. Stoler, "What Did He Really Say? The 'Aiken Formula' for Vietnam Revisited," *Vermont History* 46, 2 (1978): 100–108. Also Charles F. O'Brien, "Aiken and Vietnam: A Dialogue with Vermont Voters," *Vermont History* 61, 1 (1993), 5–17.

35. *Congressional Record,* 89th Cong., 2d sess., 1966, 112, pt. 20:27523–27525; 90th Cong., 1st sess., 1967, 113, pts. 4 and 10:4870–4871 and 12582. See also clippings in GDA Vietnam speech, crate 39, box 5, 19 October 1966 folder, Aiken Papers; Aiken letters to Henry B. Patterson, crate 39, box 5, GDA 2 May 1967 Statement folder, Aiken Papers; to Gerry Peet, 20 March 1967, crate 39, box 5, Southeast Asia 1967 Out-of-State Answered folder, Aiken Papers; and to John F. Adams and Mrs. Charles F. Cotton, 13 and 20 January 1967, crate 39, box 4, Southeast Asia Vermont Correspondence folder 1, Aiken Papers.

36. *Congressional Record,* 90th Cong., 1st sess., 1967, 113, pt. 14:18370.

37. Ibid., pt. 9:11436–11437.

38. Ibid., pt. 15:20672–20673.

39. Ibid., pts. 10, 18, and 22:12606, 24288, and 30025–30026.

40. Ibid., 2d sess., 1968, 114, pt. 1:369–371.

41. Ibid., 91st Cong., 2d sess., 1970, 116, pt. 29:38593–38595. Aiken's idea of a gradual "fade-out" was first reported in the 12 January 1966, *St. Alban's Messenger* and *Bennington Banner.* See also *Congressional Record,* 91st Cong., 1st sess., 1969, 115, pts. 8, 22, and 23:10928, 30140, and 30649–30650; David B. Wilson, "The Vermonter," *Boston Globe,* 3 November 1968, 10; Aiken speech before Wallingford Rotary Club, reported in *Rutland Herald,* 27 August 1968; Aiken to Arthur Packard, 7 May 1968, crate 39, box 6, Foreign Relations Vermont Correspondence 1968 folder, Aiken Papers.

42. Aiken speech at Norwich University, "Our Foreign Policy— Legacy of the New Deal," 1 October 1969, reprinted in *Congressional Record,* 91st Cong., 1st sess., 1969, 115, pt. 22:30140–30143. See also 93d Cong., 1st sess., 1973, 119, pt. 4: 3959–3961.

43. *Ibid.,* 91st Cong., 1st sess., 1969, 115, pts. 15–22: 20288, 22272, 26333–26335, 29103, 35907, 38467–38468, 38688–38689; 2d sess., 1970, 116, pts. 7–23:9782–9783, 10172, 10417, 10506, 17103, 19429–19430, 30665; 92d Cong., 1st sess., 1971, 117, pt.

2:2402–2404; 2d sess., 1972, 118, pts. 11–25: 14168–14169, 14636–14637, 14866, 32733; Aiken, *Senate Diary,* 45–52, 56, 58, 107–108, 145, 202; Senate Foreign Relations Committee, *Causes, Origins and Lessons of the Vietnam War,* 92d Cong., 2d sess., 1972, 33–35; crate 50, box 4, Cambodia GDA Views folder and Vietnam Troop Reduction GDA Views folder, Aiken Papers.

Chapter 8

1. *Toronto Star,* 15 January 1972.

2. Remarks at conference, "The Aiken Legacy," University of Vermont, Burlington, 25 October 1991.

3. *Congressional Record,* 77th Cong., 1st sess., 1941, 87, pt. 2:1361.

4. Crate 33, box 1, folder 19, Aiken Papers, Special Collections, Bailey/Howe Library, University of Vermont. Sharp's remark was made on 4 June 1969.

5. Ibid., crate 39, box 2, folder 16.

6. Canada, Senate, Debates, 24th Parl., 5th sess., vol. 110, no. 22, 300–301 (13 March 1962).

7. See the summary of the eleventh meeting of the Interparliamentary Group, held 19–24 March 1968, in New Orleans and Washington, D.C., crate 33, box 1, folder 18, Aiken Papers.

8. *Congressional Record,* 89th Cong., 2d sess., 1966, 112, pt. 2:1576–1577.

9. Crate 33, box 1, folder 19, Aiken Papers.

10. Ibid., folder 33.

11. Canada, House of Commons, Debates, 24th Parl., 3d sess., vol. 104, no. 89, 4271 (26 May 1960).

Chapter 9

1. Samuel B. Hand and D. Gregory Sanford, "Carrying Water on Both Shoulders: George D. Aiken's 1936 Gubernatorial Campaign in Vermont," *Vermont History* 43, 4 (1975): 292–306.

2. Published as "You Can't Get There from Here: The Presidential Boomlet for Governor George D. Aiken, 1937–1939," *Vermont History* 49, 4 (1981): 197–208.

3. "George D. Aiken Oral History Memoir," interviews by Charles T. Morrissey and D. Gregory Sanford, 1981, Folklore and Oral History Archives, Bailey/Howe Library, University of Vermont.

4. Oral history with Robert W. Mitchell, 11 March 1980, interview by D. Gregory Sanford, Special Collections, Bailey/Howe Library, University of Vermont, 2–9; oral history with Sterry R. Waterman, 13 July 1981, interview by D. Gregory Sanford, Special Collections, Bailey/Howe Library, University of Vermont, 2–42.

5. Sanford, "You Can't Get There from Here"; Mark A. Stoler, "What Did He Really Say? The 'Aiken Formula' for Vietnam Revisited," *Vermont History* 46, 2 (1978): 100–108; Mark A. Stoler, "Aiken, Mansfield, and the Tonkin Gulf Crisis: Notes from the Congressional Leadership Meeting at the White House, August 4, 1964," *Vermont History* 50, 2 (1982): 80–94. See Chapter 7 of this volume.

Chapter 10

1. Frederick J. Fayette, a Democrat, was a member of the Vermont House of Representatives for South Burlington in 1947 and 1949 and a senator for Chittenden County in 1957 and 1963 and for Chittenden and Grand Isle in 1966 and 1971–1972. He ran unsuccessfully for the U.S. Senate against Republican Winston Prouty in 1958 and 1964. He was a longtime advocate for a state power authority in Vermont.

2. Theodore M. Riehle Jr., a Republican, was a member of the Vermont House of Representatives for South Burlington from 1966 to 1967. He was state planning officer in 1968–1971.

Chapter 11

1. Sterry Waterman, a St. Johnsbury attorney, was a judge on the federal court from 1955 to 1982. Leon Latham of Burlington was an adviser to Aiken during his governorship. Winston Prouty of Newport served in the Vermont House of Representatives from 1943 to 1949 and in the U.S. House from 1951 to 1959. Peter Bove, an attorney from Rutland, made an unsuccessful bid for the Republican nomination in the 1950 gubernatorial primary. A. Luke Crispe lost in the 1960 Republican gubernatorial primary; he created the Vermont Independent

party as a way for Republicans to vote for Democrat Phil Hoff and defeat the conservative wing of the state Republican party.

2. Goldfine was a Boston textile manufacturer and real estate operator whose friendships with and lavish gifts to political figures led to a congressional investigation in 1958.

Selected Bibliography

Aiken, George D. *Aiken: Senate Diary, January 1972–January 1975.* Brattleboro, Vt.: Stephen Greene Press, 1976.

———— *Pioneering with Fruits and Berries.* Brattleboro, Vt.: Stephen Daye Press, 1936.

———— *Pioneering with Wildflowers.* New York: Stephen Daye Press, 1933. Reprint, Brattleboro, Vt.: Alan C. Hood Jr., 1994.

———— *Speaking from Vermont.* New York: Frederick A. Stokes, 1938.

"George D. Aiken Oral History Memoir." Interviews by Charles T. Morrissey and D. Gregory Sanford. Folklore and Oral History Archives, Bailey/Howe Library, University of Vermont, 1981.

George D. Aiken Papers Inventory of Collection in the Special Collections, Bailey/Howe Library, University of Vermont.

Cordtz, Dan. "Vermont's Aiken." *Wall Street Journal,* 3 March 1966, 14.

Hand, Samuel B. *Friends, Neighbors and Political Allies: Reflections on the Aiken-Gibson Connection.* Burlington: Center for Research on Vermont, 1986.

Hand, Samuel B., and D. Gregory Sanford. "Carrying Water on Both Shoulders: George D. Aiken's 1936 Gubernatorial Campaign in Vermont." *Vermont History* 43, 4 (1975): 292–306.

Hand, Samuel B., and Paul M. Searls. "Transition Politics: Vermont, 1940–1952." *Vermont History* 62, 1 (1994): 5–25.

Herbers, John. "Occupation: Farmer, Avocation: Senator." *New York Times Magazine,* 29 January 1967, 30.

Judd, Richard. *The New Deal in Vermont: Its Impact and Aftermath.* New York: Garland, 1979.

Leuchtenburg, William E. *Flood Control Politics: The Connecticut River Valley Problem, 1927–1950.* Cambridge: Harvard University Press, 1953.

O'Brien, Charles F. "Aiken and Vietnam: A Dialogue with Vermont Voters." *Vermont History* 61, 1 (1993): 5–17.

Sanford, D. Gregory. "You Can't Get There from Here: The Presidential Boomlet for Governor George D. Aiken, 1937–1939." *Vermont History* 49, 4 (1981): 197–208.

Searls, Paul M. "George Aiken and the Taft Hartley Act." *Vermont History* 60, 3 (1992): 155–166.

Stoler, Mark A. "Aiken, Mansfield, and the Tonkin Gulf Crisis: Notes from the Congressional Leadership Meeting at the White House, August 4, 1964." *Vermont History* 50, 2 (1982): 80–94.

———."What Did He Really Say? The 'Aiken Formula' for Vietnam Revisited." *Vermont History* 46, 2 (1978): 100–108.

U.S. Senate. Committee on Foreign Relations. *The Vietnam Conflict: The Substance and the Shadow.* Washington, D.C.: U.S. Government Printing Office, 1966.

A Brief Biography of
George D. Aiken

Born:
August 20, 1892, in Dummerston, Vermont, to Edward W. and Myra A. (Cook) Aiken

Died:
November 19, 1984, in Montpelier, Vermont

Education:
common schools of Putney, Vermont
graduate of Brattleboro High School, 1909
Hon. LL.D., University of Vermont, 1937
Hon. D.Sc., Norwich University, 1937

Married:
first wife: Beatrice Howard Aiken, m. 1914; d. 1966
second wife: Lola Pierotti Aiken, m. 1967

Early public career:
Became master of Putney Grange at age eighteen, 1910
Helped organize the Windham County Farm Bureau, the second to be founded in Vermont, 1913; president of the bureau in 1935 and 1936
President of the Vermont Horticultural Society, 1917–1918

School director, Town of Putney 1920–1937

Politics:

Town representative, 1931–1935

Speaker of the Vermont House of Representatives,
1933–1935

Lieutenant governor of Vermont, 1935–1937

Governor of Vermont, 1937–1941

U.S. senator, elected November 1940 to fill the unexpired
term of Ernest W. Gibson; reelected 1944, 1950, 1956,
1962, and 1968; did not seek reelection in 1974 and
retired January 1975

Committees:

Senate Committee on Civil Service, 1941–1947

Senate Committee on Pensions, 1941–1947

Senate Committee on Expenditures in the Executive
Departments, 1941–1949; chairman, 1947–1948

Senate Committee on Education and Labor, 1941–1954;
chairman, Subcommittee on Education, 1947–1948

Senate Committee on Agriculture and Forestry, 1941–1975.
Acting chairman when Senator Arthur Capper of
Kansas was unable to assume duties because of illness,
1947–1948; chairman, 1953–1954

Senate Subcommittee on Agriculture Appropriations,
1947–1971

Senate Committee on Foreign Relations, 1954–1975

Chairman of Subcommittee on Canada, 1958–1969

Joint Committee on Atomic Energy, 1959–1975

Senate Republican Policy Committee, 1959–1962,
1967–1968

Joint Committee on Republican Principles, 1962

Senate Republican Campaign Committee, 1963–1964

Senate Committee on Aeronautical and Space Sciences,
1965–1966

About the Editor and Contributors

SAMUEL B. HAND is professor of history emeritus at the University of Vermont. He is a member of the Aiken Lecture Series board of directors and has authored and coauthored several articles on George D. Aiken's political career.

PHILIP H. HOFF is a partner in the law firm of Hoff, Curtis, Pacht, Cassidy & Frame and president of the board of trustees of the Vermont Law School. Long active in state and national politics, he was the first Democrat elected governor of Vermont since before the Civil War. In addition to serving three terms as governor (1963–1969), he was Burlington's representative to the Vermont General Assembly (1961–1962) and a state senator (1983–1988).

ANNA KASTEN NELSON, a professor of history at the American University in Washington, D.C., has been a consultant to the Congressional Research Service and the Select Committee on Congressional Operations and was on the staff of the Public Documents Commission. She is currently one of five presidential appointees to the Kennedy Assassination Records Review Board.

Her most recent research focuses on the origins of the National Security Council.

JAMES L. OAKES, a former attorney general of Vermont (1967–1969) and U.S. district judge (1970–1971), was chief judge on the U.S. Court of Appeals, Second Circuit, from 1989 to 1992. He continues to serve as senior judge for the court.

CHARLES F. O'BRIEN is associate professor of history and former chair of the Department of Social Sciences at Clarkson University. He has written a number of articles on U.S.-Canadian relations, especially with regard to Lake Champlain and the St. Lawrence Seaway.

HERBERT S. PARMET, Distinguished Professor of History at Queensborough Community College and the Graduate School of the City University of New York, is the author of books on Richard Nixon, John F. Kennedy, and Dwight D. Eisenhower and articles on American political parties.

THOMAS G. PATERSON is professor of history at the University of Connecticut and a past president of the Society for Historians of American Foreign Relations. His books include *Meeting the Communist Threat, On Every Front: The Making and Unmaking of the Cold War,* and *Contesting Castro.* He has been a Guggenheim fellow and has lectured throughout the United States, as well as in Venezuela, China, and Russia.

DONALD A. RITCHIE is associate historian in the Senate Historical Office, where he conducts an oral history program and edits for publication the previously closed hearings of the Senate Foreign Relations Committee. He is an adjunct faculty member of the Cornell in Washington program and a former president of the Oral History Association. Among his books are *Press Gallery: Congress and the Washington Correspondents* and *Doing Oral History.*

D. GREGORY SANFORD has been Vermont state archivist since 1982. He was among the first students to use the Aiken papers as part of his research, writing his thesis and several articles on Aiken's career during the 1930s. He served as assistant director of the George D. Aiken Oral History Project.

MICHAEL SHERMAN is director of the Vermont Historical Society.

MARK A. STOLER has been a member of the University of Vermont history department since 1970, concentrating on twentieth-century diplomatic and military history. He has been a visiting professor at the Naval War College, the University of Haifa, and the U.S. Military Academy at West Point. He is currently completing a study of the military view of U.S. foreign policy during World War II and researching the work of Senator Aiken in foreign affairs.

STEPHEN C. TERRY is vice president and general manager of retail energy services at Green Mountain Power Corporation in South Burlington, Vermont. A former managing editor of the *Rutland Herald,* he interrupted a career in journalism to serve on George D. Aiken's legislative staff from 1969 to 1975.

JAMES WRIGHT is dean of the Faculty of Arts and Sciences at Dartmouth College, where he has served as a faculty member in the history department since 1969 and as acting president of the college for the first half of 1995. A former Guggenheim fellow, he has written books on the Populist period, progressivism, and the Republican party.

Index

Acheson, Dean, 85
Africa, 87, 153
African Americans, 138
Agriculture, 78–79. *See also* Farm
   surplus
Aid to Women, Infants, and
   Children, 150
Aiken family, 33, 145–146
Aiken, Edward, Col., 146
Aiken, Edward, Deacon, 146
Aiken, Edward W. (father), 33, 38,
   146
Aiken, George David: on Agri-
   cultural Committee, 61, 67, 76,
   78–79, 80, 119, 151; and agri-
   cultural policy, 100, 101, 119,
   149–150, 151; his ancestors, 33,
   145–146; his campaign spend-
   ing, 59–60, 130, 131, 154; and
   Canada, 117–122, 153; Winston
   Churchill's novels, influence on,
   25, 27, 32; on the CIA, 87; and
   civil rights, 19, 64–65; on Committee on Expenditures in the
   Executive Department, 75; on
   Committee on Labor and Public
   Welfare, 75; and communism,
   101–102, 102–103, 112; constituents, service to, 66, 67, 68,
70; daily work schedule, 65–70;
"declare a victory and get out" of
Vietnam, 43–44, 99, 100,
110–111, 114–115, 130, 155;
Democratic support for, 136;
diary, writing of, 65; on economy, 94–95; his education,
146–147; election to U.S.
Senate, 13, 17, 49, 154; and the
environment, 71, 151; on executive power, 16, 18–19, 102, 104,
106, 114, 154; farmer and plant
grower, 146–148, 151, 156; food
preferences, 65, 66, 68, 69; and
foreign affairs, 100–101, 114,
153; on Foreign Relations
Committee, 39, 52–54, 58, 61,
67, 76, 79–80, 100, 103, 119; as
governor, 16–17, 60, 101, 102,
118, 150, 152, 154; homes, 26,
65, 156; honorific title of
"Governor," 21; on Joint
Committee on Atomic Energy,
76, 78; on Labor Committee,
101; and McCarthyism, 34, 39;
and New Deal, 16, 17, 38, 101;
nuclear power, faith in, 78, 152;

BENNINGTON FREE LIBRARY

BENNINGTON FREE LIBRARY

NF   328.73 POL

The political legacy of Geo

3 0260 0003 0875 3

Microbial Plant Pathology